Living Alone

Choices for
Women Who are
Single Again

[handwritten inscription] To Holly & Brek — Arlene Shuster Proverbs 31:30 b

By Arlene Cook Shuster

Living Alone: Choices for Women Who are Single Again
By Arlene Cook Shuster

ISBN 978-1530514502

Published by Cook Enterprises
PO Box 458, Escondido, CA 92033
arleneshuster@cox.net

Dedicated with love to my daughter
Alyse
with admiration for the mentoring
Woman of God that she is.
She speaks with wisdom and faithful instruction.
(PROVERBS 31:26)

Table of Contents

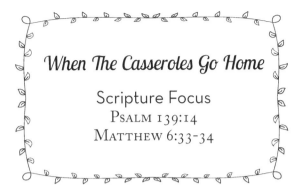

When The Casseroles Go Home

Scripture Focus
PSALM 139:14
MATTHEW 6:33-34

EACH ONE OF US remembers the day, if not the hour, our marriage ended. Whether our friends and families acknowledge the same date depends on circumstances often kept locked in our hearts.

Some may think your marriage ended when hubby ran off with his secretary. In your heart it ended years before, when you lost your baby at five months and spent three days in the hospital regaining strength from blood loss. Months later, your husband casually said in front of friends, "Pat wasn't pregnant. She probably had the flu. Putting her in the hospital was the doctor's way to gouge me for more money." That was the day you began to grieve two losses.

Another circumstance could be the day your husband had a serious stroke. You sorrowed over the irrevocably changed lover/companionship "oneness" that joyfully bound you together years ago as you two pledged before God … 'in sickness, in health until death do you part.' God's love held you both in His arms as you entered another chapter in your married life, dearly loving and caring for the earthly body that no longer resembled the man you married years ago. The day God called him home was a heart-wrenching distance from the hour you began to grieve.

For some of us, "grieving to healing" takes a long time. We all believe that we are emotionally prepared for the possible unexpected end to our marriage --the sound of the death rattle or the delivery of divorce papers. No matter how her marriage ended, I've not talked with one woman who is single again, who managed to avoid the stranglehold of sudden shock and perhaps a self-imposed burden of guilt at the moment of the certain death of her marriage.

Finally, it arrives – the day the casserole dishes go back to their owners; the day the last well-meaning relative waves good-bye. It's the day you wake-up, put your feet on the floor and step into a life of aloneness.

As unwilling and unprepared as we may feel, it is time to look to the future with the clarity that God knows "*...even the very hairs of your head are all numbered. So don't be afraid; you are worth more than many sparrows.*" (Matthew 10:30-31)

This is not a time in your life to wallow in self-pity. It is not a time to move forward with the attitude to "make the best of it." Hopefully, you were not reared by your parents to *just survive*, you were reared to *thrive*. So let's get on with your journey – together!

Whether she's the Queen of England, your favorite movie star or your best friend, lifelong joy and eternal life in God's presence only begins with accepting God's gift of faith, love and forgiveness. Let us begin with our own reaffirmation of *faith* in Jesus Christ as our personal Savior by claiming these signature Bible verses for our time together. *"Love the Lord your God with all your heart and with all your soul and with all your mind and with all your strength. The second is this: Love your neighbor as yourself. There is no commandment greater then these."* (Mark 12:30-31)

Get ready, be confident as you discover God's purpose for you. Embrace it as you would every blessing coming your way. However, be watchful, as God has a wonderful sense of humor. It's likely to appear at any time on any day without fair warning. You'll recognize it when it happens. Be ready to reach for the golden ring of an abundant life!

"You make known to me the path of life; you will fill me with joy in your presence, with eternal pleasures at your right hand." (Psalm 16:11)

Footnote: Tuck a small notepad in your purse. The first day jot down something that "happens" to brighten your outlook, direct your understanding or bring you a sense of peace. Call it the "jewel" of your day. It is a gift sent from God to remind you that He is real and that He loves you. The second day, jot down two things that touch you in a positive way, adding sparkle to your day, such as an encouraging call from a friend, or a surprise note in the mail, even a butterfly flit by. Begin to anticipate, look for your daily jewels. As you continue to open your heart to discover God's purpose for your life, your daily notations will soon fill the page. As your jewel collection grows, so will the luster return to your daily life.

Footprint: *"Thank you, Lord, for the gift of faith. Take my hand. Guide my single steps beside you so that the footprints I leave behind will lead others to honor You and bring great glory to your name. Amen"* (Isaiah 43:7)

Single Steps Beside God

Scripture Focus
JOHN 14:27
PSALM 119:76

"Let's be a comfortable couple and take care of each other! And if we should get deaf, or lame, or blind, or bedridden, how glad we shall be that we have somebody we are fond of, always to talk to and sit with! Let's be a comfortable couple. Now, do, my dear!"

Charles Dickens

COMFORTABLENESS. In a word, that is what those of us learning to live alone miss most about marriage. Remember the difficult ups and downs of the early years of marriage? It was a commitment held together in part by delirious passion, tenacity and God's gracious answer to prayer.

Some scientists believe the sheer euphoria of early love is a response to chemical substances (cousins of amphetamines) swamping the brain. They believe the meeting of the eyes, the touch of fingers, the electrifying nearness of Mr. Right, sends love-chemicals roller-coasting along the nerves and surging through the blood stream.

Researchers further contend that after a few years together, the body builds up a natural tolerance to nature's love potion. Enduring love, they contend, is due in some degree to the stepped- up production of endorphins, (chemically similar to morphine) that begin to flow into the brain. It provides partners with a comfortable sense of security, peace and calm.

However, scientists cannot explain why I was attracted to my husband in the first place. Or why, as the meeting's moderator, he noticed me, especially, from among the feminine faces in the audience. I called it a young woman's answer to prayer.

Allow yourself a moment to reminisce. Draw up that magical moment the "single you" met the man God intended as your life's partner. True love is more than chemistry, isn't it? The unity of love blessed at the altar of God has greater depth than the co-mingling of wind and rain, dreams and reality, poetry and orange-blossom promises. A commitment "until death do us part" and "let no man put asunder" are pledges in harmony with God's plan for our lives. Now that sense of harmony is gone.

Whether by death or divorce, the loss of couple-companionship, safe-keeping, along with adjusting to the lifestyle of living alone can be more difficult to cope with than the initial loss of a spouse. It can take longer and cost more in emotional energy, while devastating our fragile self-confidence in the process.

We may not be able to control where we are at this moment of loss, but we can control who we want to be. Reach out, accept our return to singleness as a new beginning, an opportunity to become reacquainted with the wondrous *me* God created and fashioned to do His good works. (Psalm 139:14)

Before we can experience heartfelt happiness again, before we can again be the caring, sharing, resourceful and fulfilled women God intends, we need to recall something more.

God, who brought us our one-true-love is *The Comforter* of us all. His unfailing love will be our comfort. His promise will bring joy into our lives once again. Come, walk with me. Our journey beside God begins with a single step.

Footnote: Join me in claiming God's promise for victory in our new lifestyle. I can do everything through Him who gives me strength. (Philippians 4:13)

Footprint: *Thank you, Lord, for Your comforting arms wrapped closely around me. Remind me daily, that I can do all things through You. Guide my single steps so that the footprints I leave behind will honor You with a new maturity. Amen.*

Time-Dated Material

Scripture Focus
1 THESSALONIANS 5:2
ROMANS 15:13

HAVE YOU EVER KNOWN JUNK MAIL to deliver a first-class message? I certainly hadn't – until this morning.

I was sorting a stack of incoming mail, when I came across a feminine-looking envelope carrying the bold imprint **"Time-Dated Material Enclosed."** I sent the envelope airmailing toward the trash basket before I realized the personal importance of that catchy sales pitch.

I retrieved the piece of mail and noticed the bulk-mailing permit. Women everywhere were getting the same message, virtually at no cost to themselves. Yet, I doubt many will "get the message" and act on it.

To me, "time-dated material," means *"I'm important. I'm worth a second look. Now!"* The second bold-print line read **"This Offer Has A Deadline!"**

My psyche feels stamped-on, stapled through and generally mutilated by the recent events in my world. I could use a reminder that I'm worth checking out, now!

It's time for me to take a peek inside me and make an assessment of my first-class contents. I have unique talents and skills that God "special-delivered" to me the moment I was born. I have attributes and opportunities I have yet to open and explore.

Lois, my recently widowed friend, prioritized my thinking when she shared, "My dear Alfred fought so long and hard for his life, I dare not be cavalier about my own. I intend to honor our many years together by making the most of each of my remaining days."

Lois has accepted what we each know instinctively. Each of us has an unannounced deadline to our love and outreach on earth before our "return to sender." God promises me peace and joy. It's mine. It's free for the asking. Immediate home delivery is guaranteed!

The star route to God's promise is found in His Word. It, too, is time-dated material. The Bible is the book that God commands us to "open at once," as it contains the most important message ever sent. Its precious content, its eternal value, has a definite deadline for acceptance. That deadline is clearly announced. It coincides exactly with my "return to sender" date.

I'm time-dated. So are you!

Footnote: How would you spend today if you knew tomorrow you would be "returned to sender?"

Footprint: *Lord, I know You are my Creator. You sent me into this world carrying your stamp of approval, blessed with the capacity to know peace and joy through You. You equipped me with the potential to do great things. Teach me, Lord, to live for You — live each day as if it were my last on earth. Amen.*

A Place Where God Speaks

Scripture Focus
PSALM 62:1
MARK 9:7

WHERE DID YOU GO TO PRAY ALONE when you were a little girl? Don't count bedtime prayers rattled off in unison with sisters who shared the same sleeping space. That is not being alone with God.

Our home sat among an outcropping of large granite boulders along the ridge that divided our small town to the west from the country groves and farms to the east. Behind our vintage WW11 small house was a split rock taller than I was, with a deep crevice cut to the ground. I could stretch out on my stomach and watch the tiny cars below move about the town's roads like ants on patrol.

That secret hide-away became my prayer place, a place where I could sneak away and tell God everything. I could watch the miniature street lights flicker alive at dusk, while waiting for God to talk to me.

Looking back, I think I expected always to have a prayer place and the time to talk with God. But then, I was a child and thought as a child.

My prayer place in college was a maze of cross-campus sidewalks. I remember praying semi-aloud on the run to class.

"Lord, help me remember the formula", or *"God, give me total recall for the test."* There was little time to wait on God's counsel.

I'm certain God wanted equal time. He longed to be heard as much as I did. I look back and marvel at His patience with me.

When my children were pre-teenagers, we spent a week each summer with other church families camping at Carlsbad State Beach. I looked forward to the scent of sea air washing over me, mellowing every taut nerve ending in my body.

One sunset, while all the camp kids were playing board games, I excused myself to take a solitary stroll down the beach. It wasn't long before I was pouring out my heart to God. Then I walked along in silence, watching my footprints sink deeper into the wet sand with each step. That's when I started to listen, as I had done as a child.

By the time I reached the caves, carved out by eons of thrashing surf, the high tide was lapping at my ankles. I was as far as I could go safely.

I turned back toward our vacation trailers in the distance, perched on the bluffs over-looking the Pacific Ocean. I watched for the "green flash" as the sun disappeared completely below the horizon. By now, God and I were in a two-way conversation. Why had I allowed the prayer place in my heart to slip away to a one-way soap box? And for so long!

Selecting a prayer place presents a unique opportunity. Make it a refuge free of distraction, special and comfortable. A place you'd meet your heart of hearts friend. That's who you are meeting, after all.

My friend, Carolyn, who has been alone for years, has made the potting shed behind her house a private sanctuary. The smell of damp, nurtured soil provides an emotional shelter for her mind. "Here," she says, *"Truly, my soul silently waits for God."* (Psalm 62:1)

Phyllis lives in a small mobile home. It's decorated reminiscent of her stay in Germany. Lace curtains at the windows filter the morning light. Near the corner window is a shawl-draped recliner. A side table holds a flowering African violet warmed by the sun. A worn Bible rests within reach. Phyllis pointed, "Here's where I meet God at sunrise. Here is where He gives me my challenges for the day."

After we returned from our beach holiday, I searched for a grown-up, quiet place of my own. I found it in my breakfast nook, in front of the bay window. Outside is a pecan tree, visited often by blue jays and woodpeckers. Family pictures hang on every wall. I meet God over tea and prayer.

He reaches down, touches the dawn of my "renewed" commitment, filling my cup with His love and His direction on how I can give my best to the day. I listen.

Footnote: Where do you go to God in prayer and conversation. Do you give Him a chance to get a word in?

Footprint: *"Be still before the Lord and wait patiently for Him"* (Psalm 37:7a)

Listen To Your Body

Scripture Focus
PHILIPPIANS 4:6
1 CORINTHIANS 6:19-20

"YOU CAN READ HER LIKE A BOOK." Remember that old adage? God takes care of us, but He also expects us to take care of ourselves. He expects *me* to learn to read *myself* like a book.

For instance, when I reach stress overload, a cup of hot tea turns to molten lava in my stomach. My body is telling me that I am in over my head. I immediately ask myself, "What do I need to change?" To ignore my body's warning is to invite a stomach ulcer. For those of us prone to stress overload, the result could be chronic headaches, heart disease, anxiety or something worse.

Barbara's aching shoulders signal that the burden she is carrying is too heavy. Cynthia's frequent headaches flash emotional overload. Both women have choices. Both have the opportunity to listen to their bodies and re-prioritize their concerns, expectations and schedules.

Good health is a gift, more so as we grow older. To "tough it out" in pain or anguish is not being brave, it's being foolish. There's little hope of fulfilling God's aspirations for us as Christian women when we are hurting.

According to the latest medical findings, stress *overload* and stress *underload* are responsible for 80% to 90% of all illnesses. We survivors of a recent divorce, or death of a spouse, are painfully aware that our "stress temperature" may have rocketed beyond normal limits. With God's guidance we can help stabilize our emotional temperature.

Even if we are forewarned, death or divorce, when it hits, barrels like a shock wave through our body's systems, leaving behind a backwash of depression, digestive disturbances and debilitating our best thinking. Caregivers face a significantly higher risk of heart attack during the week following a loved one's death, according to a study published in the journal *Circulation*.

Stress management is not the process of ridding ourselves of all stress. There's good stress, the kind that stimulates our brain and body to reach for the stars.

In order to remain healthy and productive during these difficult days of adapting to aloneness, we each must sort out the stresses that gnaw at our insides and sap our strength.

If life is losing its luster, stop and assess where you really are and where you want to end up. Ask yourself, "To what purpose in life am I called? Do I fully appreciate my God-given uniqueness?

Does my faith include a daily commitment to a Christ-pleasing lifestyle?" It's time to check on your "faith thermometer."

Here are proven ways to help with stress overload, including the lowering of your bad cholesterol numbers.

Prayer, meditation: both force us to slow down, breathe deeply and gain a fresh perspective by listening to God.

Laugh: You may not feel in the mood for a chuckle, but that's exactly what the doctor orders. Laughter may undo the effects of stress by flooding your body with relaxing chemicals.

Food Choices: We all have a tendency to run to junk foods during times of stress. It can become a vicious circle. That's not a time we remember that grains and sugar are our enemies.

The right diet can undo stress, leaving us feeling calmer, happier and more energetic. Let's get to the list of good foods for our bodies. You'll love some of the "happy" making choices: green leafy vegetables – eat a variety, eat plenty – they are reported to be super depression fighters.

Here are a more food choices to help keep you in a better frame of mind – organic turkey breast and pumpkin seeds. The beneficial bacteria found in certain yogurts helps improve brain function. I'm for that!

Wild-caught salmon plays an important role in emotional well-being, according to several studies I researched. Blueberries reportedly helps memory function beside all the health benefits we've heard about in the last few years. Eating two servings of pistachios a day is reported to lower vascular constriction during stress. Now for the surprise for most of us – dark chocolate has been referred to by some as the "new anti-anxiety drug." You can sink your teeth into this sweet treat without an ounce of guilt. What a lovely way to become calmer!

Nor do I need to feel guilty eating a half of an avocado for lunch! Avocados provide almost 20 essential health-boosting nutrients and this delicious fruit is gaining a reputation of satisfying us, keeping us from the temptation to snack later in the afternoon. Of course, there are many other healthy choices within our reach. Explore on your own. Also, as our mothers taught us, drink plenty of water during the day. Drinking a glass of water 20 minutes before a meal helps take the edge off hunger. Thus, we eat a little less at mealtime.

Exercise: Most of us grimace at this one. First choice: sign up for a water aerobics class at a local fitness center or YMCA. Water exercise provides a sense of freedom, beside the bonus of possible weight loss. A note from personal experience – indoor pool air can transport all kinds of airborne germs, bacteria and viruses. Outdoor pools may have cooler air temperatures, but know this, the cooler the air, the warmer the water feels.

Swimming is good exercise for your blood vessels, allowing them to relax and be less of a reactor to stress. It's a blue ribbon exercise for diabetics.

Second choice would be a daily long walk. Invite a friend or neighbor to join you. You'll amaze yourself on how much farther you'll comfortably walk. Increase your distance and time a little each time you walk. Chat about anything except you and your troubles. Keep it light!

Sleep: sleep is crucial for heart health and the ability to manage stress. Check with your doctor if you are a troubled sleeper. I like going to bed with a good book. I look forward to it.

Part of learning to "read" oneself is realizing that stress is not pressure from the outside. It is the physical reaction within our bodies to what we perceive as threatening situations. Realize too, that these first days of adapting may seem long, dark. We can shorten and lighten the journey simply by changing our perception of events.

For example, the next time your car won't start and you know you will be late to church, don't concern yourself about what others will think when you walk into the service half way through the sermon. Accept at the first moment, that God has a better plan for you. Put this incident in His hands.

Perhaps, your church time will be better spent witnessing to the AAA service man. You may never know, had you started out for church, you may have collided with a drunk driver. Only God knows. Trust your day to Him.

Footnote: Ask yourself, "What changes do I need to make to take care of me?" Ask God through prayer. Listen for His answer.

Footprint: *"Listen to my advice and be wise; do not ignore it."* (Proverbs 8:33)

Movie Of The Week

Scripture Focus
PROVERBS 3:5
MATTHEW 11:28

SUSAN, SEPARATED ONLY A FEW MONTHS after their silver anniversary celebration, was acutely sensitive to the pain of singleness, which to her was synonymous with loneliness.

She called one dark, rainy Saturday afternoon in a voice that was as empty as an echo chamber. I suggested that we get out and drive to nearby Rancho Bernardo for a light supper and then check out the new movie theater.

We arrived early at the theater and settled down in the back row for a few minutes of people-watching. After a little while, Susan nudged me and whispered, "See that woman sitting alone two rows down on the other side of the aisle? Isn't she attractive?"

Before I could get a good look at the woman, other than her profile, a man strode down the aisle and stopped at her row. He glanced our way as he sat down next to the woman. He saw us. It was Susan's husband!

Just then, the house lights dimmed. Susan's husband, awkwardly shielding his companion from view, hurriedly left the theater under the cover of darkness.

I caught my breath as I felt my blood start to boil. I turned to Susan. The glint of a tear trickled down her cheek. She smiled heroically and whispered, "I'm okay. In shock, but okay." She squeezed my hand reassuringly.

On the way home, Susan raised the subject on her own. "I knew she existed," she started slowly, her voice thin. "Our next door neighbors introduced them to one another only two weeks after he moved out. The Millers told me that Mark seemed so lonely. As if he was the only one!"

Susan wiped away a tear and continued. "Until tonight, I was as angry with my neighbors as I was with Mark. They didn't allow our separation to do its work before they put their noses in our marriage. I felt they had interfered with God's plan."

"After you saw them together tonight..?"

"I didn't see them as "together." I saw a man who is still angry, still hurting. I saw a man who is not proud of what he is doing, a man struggling with guilt. Mark's is as lonely as I am. God has a plan for our marriage. I need to trust God's timing for a resolution. I need to trust that resolution."

There are ways to cope with lonely times when you feel alone, while you wait on God. Try playing mix-and-match. List five activities you might like to do on a dark, rainy afternoon, such as playing Scrabble, working a jig-saw puzzle, grabbing an upbeat movie, keeping a reservation at a tea room or making chili and sourdough biscuits.

List five women single women friends who would enjoy one or more of your chosen activities. Mix-and-match a friend with an activity to fit your mood. Most important – follow through! Make a telephone call in a cheery voice.

Footnote: How often have we heard "let go and let God?" Only God knows how much weight each of us will stubbornly carry before we fall on our knees and ask God for His resolution to our problems.

Footprint: *Lord, teach me to wait on You and not expect miracles from others. Amen.*

Remain Standing, Please!

Scripture Focus
Psalm 31:3
Matthew 26:41

It happened quickly – and in my own home! One moment I was at the top of the stairs starting down, the next moment I was airborne, tumbling headfirst. My greatest fear was not of possible injuries, but of being alone and unable to call for help.

I landed on the bottom step in an awkward sprawl, my new image-splitting bifocals still in place! A quick inventory revealed that I was fine, despite a scraped elbow, sore knee and a case of shakes over what could have been.

I might have ended up like Maggie, my physically-fit neighbor. She slipped off the back step five months ago and is still confined to bed in a skilled nursing facility waiting for a shattered femur to knit. (*Thank you, Lord, for Maggie's sound mind and patient spirit.*)

Those of us who live alone should look closely at a sobering statistic -- falls are a major cause of disability or death for older adults. With farsighted care we can dramatically improve our chances for personal and home safety.

Personal Safety

Most falls are caused by slippery floors, throw rugs and icy sidewalks. Wet leaves and grass are also dangerous. There are an abundance of stylish, low-heeled and sandal gripper-soled shoes on the market, especially for online or catalog shoppers. A household pet may be a good companion, unless it's one that keeps close company with your legs. We naturally shift our center of balance when carrying a full laundry basket or bags of groceries. Learn to kick off your high-heeled shoes before toting anything heavy up or down stairs.

Inner ear infections or prescription drugs may impair one's balance. Check with your doctor if either applies to you.

It would be wise to discuss hormone therapy with your family doctor. It's one of the preventions against osteoporosis, the brittle-bone disease that causes bones to fracture before you fall. As an added bonus, hormone therapy helps keep post-menopausal emotions in balance. Wear a necklace alarm, when pressed, it will alert a central station. Whether outside gardening or doing household chores indoors, you'll not feel alone.

Falls can occur when one's blood pressure changes abruptly due to change in position, such as getting up suddenly from a chair or in the middle of the night to use the bathroom. Baggy sleeves, bracelets and rings can catch on doorknobs and banisters as easily as overlong pants or ankle length nightgowns can trip you up.

Vanity is out-of-fashion. Have your hearing and vision tested on a regular basis. If you need help, get it. Sharp eyes and ears are your best warning to the dangers of high curbs, icy or uneven sidewalks and approaching traffic. (I was good to myself. I exchanged my distracting bifocals for ungraded Verilux lenses.)

Checklist for Home Safety

Floors: roll up your throw rugs and stuff them somewhere. They can be your worst enemy. Securely fasten worn carpet edges, loose floor boards and trailing electrical wires.

Bathrooms: Add grab bars in tub and shower enclosures. Install high-rise low-flow toilets. Apply colorful nonskid decals on shower and tub floors. Use nonskid bath mats.

Lighting: Switches should be within easy reach, including those in the garage. Install light switches at the top and bottom of stairways and night-lights in hallways and bathroom. Repair sidewalk bulges and cracks. Make certain all walkways are well-lighted. Add outdoor motion lights if possible.

Footprint: Thinking of changing addresses? Make up a safety checklist before scouting for a new residence. Do not trade safety for amenities.

Both are possible in the same address. Have patience in your search. God bless home safe home!

Footprint: *Dear Jesus, send a holy angel to protect me throughout my busy day. Keep me from falling into harm's way and bless me with the courage to stand up for You! Amen.*

The Vantage Point

Scripture Focus
PSALM 13:5
ROMANS 15:13

WE HEARD IT AT THE SAME MOMENT – the far-off sound of a wooden spoon banging against Oma's heavy stock pot.

My younger sister, Phyllis, and I tumbled out of our grandmother's guest roll-away bed and raced in to the enclosed sun porch. We climbed up on the overstuffed couch and pressed our noses against an icy window pane.

From our perch, we could see Oma outside on the stoop, shivering in the cold, one step above the frost-covered lawn. At first glance, she looked as foreign as her heavy German accent sounded. Oma was wrapped in a blue plaid wool robe, her loosened hair draped like a grey shawl halfway down her back.

Our petite, wrinkle-faced grandmother had other observers as well. Wild birds, sporting heavy coats and bright vests, toe-danced on the barren tree branches bordering the backyard. Most were immigrants like Oma. They tossed cautious, sur-veilling glances in her direction.

"Come, come, have faith. Don't be afraid." We heard her call as she cast dollops of warm, grainy gruel toward the icicle-crusted bushes. Finally one, then another morning visitor, swooped down to snatch a quick bite.

I am now the same age as my widowed grand-mother was years ago, when I peeked at her through the icy window pane. Only now, I see her witness clearly. I'm able to focus less on her "peculiar" speech and more on my memory of her trust in the cross of Jesus.

I am able to reflect on the loneliness she must have felt as a young woman boarding the ship that was to carry her to "the promised land." She told me once that childhood memories of her fami-ly's good times together gave wings to her spirit. Why do I allow bitter memories to sadden mine?

The language barrier Oma encountered did not keep her from reaching out in God's love to feed others. What barrier keeps me from stepping out to serve others?

To those of us learning to live alone, the unchart-ed seas ahead can appear dark, foreboding. What if my grandmother had panicked and turned away from the boarding ramp?

Much of our inspiration is within the reach of loving arms. Why did I have to find myself lonely before I discovered that I've never really been alone? Not only is God's umbrella protecting me, His son covers me with His love and forgiveness. We all have earthly family and/or friends, if not members of the animal kingdom who yearn for our love. From my vantage point, I see many places to give and receive love.

Footnote: Think about women alone, who have inspired you to reach out to others. How did each one's faith demonstrate courage in coping?

Footprint: *"I am trusting Thee to guide me; Thou alone shalt lead, Ev-'ry day and hour supplying All my need."*

"I Am Trusting Thee, Lord Jesus"
Frances R. Havergal, 1874

When A Hang Up Is The Best Answer

Scripture Focus
PSALM 27:1
PSALM 23:1

I REACHED THE TELEPHONE on the second ring. "May I speak to your husband? I owe him an apology," the well-spoken young male caller began.

I have a cell phone, but keep my unlisted landline because I have a FAX machine which requires it. The landline is also tied into my security alarm company.

I didn't recognize the voice. I replied cautiously, "He is unavailable at the moment. Who's calling please?

Without answering my question, he took control by saying, "I actually owe you the apology. Last night, my car broke down in your neighborhood. I took a short-cut home by climbing your back fence and crossing your patio. Your bedroom shade was up. I watched you undress. Your nakedness, your…"

I slammed down the receiver. My body shook with cross-currents of rage and humiliation. The obscene caller had my number and had been tricked into telling him I was alone. Where was he? Had he really watched me undress? Would my "hang-up" incite him to lie in wait for me? Today? Tomorrow? In less than two minutes he had shattered my emotional security and violated the privacy of my sanctuary.

I know God watches over me. I also know that He intends for me to exercise my God-given abilities to protect myself. Each crisis builds character and strengthens confidence, I reminded myself. Like most of us, I feel more secure when armed with facts. I began my research with a call to Dr. William Gordon.

Dr. William Gordon, for years a psychiatrist at California Men's Colony, told me "The man who makes obscene calls usually has a history of exhibitionism, window peeping, rape and sometimes rape-murder. Even if only 30 per cent of obscene callers are preparing for the act of rape, a woman still can't know the depth of rage of the caller harassing her."

Dr. Bill Mossman, veteran criminal psychologist, stated that almost every rapist-murderer on death row has obscene telephone calling as part of his bag of tricks. The probability of a caller seeking out and raping the woman he repeatedly calls, multiplies with each telephone contact.

Both professionals insist the best way to discourage an obscene caller is to hang up! Do not question, berate, tease or read the Bible to him. Do not incur his wrath by blowing a whistle in his ear. Simply and silently hang up!

Secondly, report every call to the police and to the telephone company. Most likely, you are not the only woman in town receiving such calls. Each report adds a piece to the puzzle, helping identify the criminal victimizing an area.

After the third call, insist the telephone carrier install a trap on your line. If the carrier refuses, notify the Public Utilities Commission. You are entitled to privacy and protection in your home.

Without thinking it through, some women simply get a new hardline or cell phone number. That may not be the wisest choice. In today's internet world, the serious caller will have your address. You may be exchanging a telephone ring for a doorbell ring.

Remember, cyber space travels both directions. The authorities can most likely zero in on the unsuspecting stalker, freeing you and possible other victims from fear.

Footnote: Remember to keep an open line to God. He is on-call twenty-four hours a day to answer prayers of thanksgiving, as well as to listen to prayer for protection.

Footprint: *"Call upon Me in the day of trouble: I shall rescue you, and you will honor Me."* (Psalm 50:15)

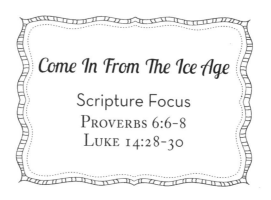

Come In From The Ice Age

Scripture Focus
PROVERBS 6:6-8
LUKE 14:28-30

IT WAS A LAZY SUMMER AFTERNOON at the beach. The four of us, protected by sun screen, broad-brimmed straw hats and dark glasses, slumped comfortably in a row of low-slung beach chairs facing the surf.

Keeping watchful eyes on our youngsters riding the breakers, we chatted and caught up on our reading. Once in awhile, one of us would read aloud something unusually funny or perhaps controversial.

"Do you know your own business?" Dorothy inquired aloud, reading the first line from an article by the same title. That question sparked a conversation among us I've not forgotten in the quarter century since that surfside afternoon.

"My husband pays the bills. That's his department," Edie offered. I don't know who we owe, or how much we pay for anything." She pushed her glasses higher on her nose. "It's his job to provide," she added a bit haughtily.

Dorothy, an office bookkeeper, jumped in, "The article says that seven out of ten of us will outlive our husbands." She dropped the magazine and offered, "You'd be surprised how many women in this day and age don't know how to write a check or balance a bank statement."

Peggy laughed. "When I need grocery money, I hold out my hand. Larry doles out the cash I ask for. I've got enough to think about managing the home and the kids."

Dorothy was flabbergasted. "Peggy! How would you handle your monthly income and expenses if something happened to Larry? Do you know how to make a budget?"

Peggy confessed, sighing, "Larry finally gave up asking me the same question. As I tell him, 'I would close the business and trust God with the next step.' The subject is morbid. Larry's not going to die until we are old. We've lots of time ahead to deal with it."

Very few of us have Peggy's archaic attitude. However, the truth is that most women our age are unprepared to handle more money than the cash in our wallets. We are remnants of an era when women commonly were isolated from the reality of family finances. It's up to those of us with frosty hair to come in from the Ice Age and join our daughters in the electronic age, including learning the basics of personal financial planning!

Peggy was correct, we should trust God, who is the source of all that we have. However, God expects something from us. He expects us to be good stewards of our monetary blessings. Haven't we read enough parables in the Bible about stewardship? Or, did we think conserving God's gifts were lessons for only those living when Christ walked the earth?

Remember the story of Joseph? He set aside a saving account of seven years resources *before* he was faced with seven years of hard times. (Genesis 41: 46-57)

King David collected money to build the temple *before* he assigned Solomon the task of construction. (1 Kings.)

Whether we need to acquire, or brush up on basic budgeting skills, the challenge is formidable. It's no secret, most women left alone, for whatever reason, usually face a drastic cut in monthly income.

Balancing a budget is the first step in personal financial planning. Budgeting simply means deciding ahead of time how much money is to be paid, and to whom, from the money available. When the money is gone, it's gone. Budget wisely.

Begin the process by asking, "How much net income do I have coming in this month?" Then list the month's expected expenses in order of priority – tithe, rent or mortgage, utilities, phone, gasoline and food. Be sure to include one-twelfth of the costs of all yearly insurances, including health supplements, taxes, licenses, and car repair bills. If you are holding any debt, add that expense and any others unique to your situation.

How about savings? Try to build an emergency fund equivalent to three six months income. Do not use your nest egg to make extra payments on debt.

Plan ahead for big budget items – a new car, vacation in the islands or your own version of Solomon's temple. Budgeting pays rich rewards. The icing on the cake is greater confidence in one's financial situation and the freedom to enjoy the fruits of your labors since the Ice Age.

Footnote: How are you spending your treasure? Make a budget and find out. Need to make any changes?

Footprint: *"For where your treasure is, there your heart will be also."* (Matthew 6:21b)

Title Goes Here

Scripture Focus
COLOSSIANS 3:12-17
MATTHEW 7:20

ACCORDING TO ETIQUETTE, a woman is a "Miss" until she marries. Earlier in my adulthood, a married woman was a "Mrs." widowed or not, until she died.

Several events collided in the early 1970's, sparking the moniker revolution of the century. Divorce statistics raced skyward and longevity tables indicated wives outlive their husbands by an average of 15 years. More women alone filtered back into their professions, more women alone returned to the work force for economic reasons. It was the time when women began to yearn for "truth in labeling" for themselves.

Women's rights advocates have taken credit for promoting the title of "Ms" among women who are unattached to a man. The movement moved from trend to tradition with the success of *Ms Magazine*, and the slow emergence of "Ms" as a definer on credit applications, doctor's records and government agencies, including the US Passport Office.

At first, many divorced women rejected the "Ms" title. It was an indelible tattoo that stamped "marriage failed" atop the already heavy, and some considered shameful, burden they carried.

That is no longer the case. Over time, divorcees, widows, most unmarried and a fair number of married women consider "Ms" a respectable alternate moniker. Fortunately, the "grass widow" tag for divorcees in our grandmothers' day, no longer exists in today's society. In truth, "Ms" accords women the cloak of privacy that has been accorded men for centuries in the title "Mr."

Choosing from among "Mrs." "Miss" and "Ms" is one of the first steps you and I take as a woman alone. And blessedly, we are free to change our minds!

Lest we allow this opportunity for free choice to go to our heads, remember, it is the title *others* give us that becomes our legacy. Fair or not, when we are no longer a couple, it is often necessary for a woman to start afresh to build a respectable name for herself.

Christ knows our every need and desire. He tells us to clothe ourselves in compassion, kindness, humility, gentleness and patience for a new life in Him. He tells us that we will be known by our fruits.

When I filled out my first credit application as a woman alone, I daringly checked the "Ms" box on the first line. I felt a sense of emancipation. I realized then that I liked being my own person. I liked being me!

Footnote: Think of at least five women whom the world has titled for their close walk beside God. You may count Joan of Arc as one.

Footprint: *Thank you, Lord, for the Bible, Your inspired guide to daily living. I pray that growing in and through your Word, I earn the title "Spirit-Filled Woman of God." Amen*

Clutter Control

Scripture Focus
COLOSSIANS 2:5
MATTHEW 12:43-45

"WHERE IS THAT JAR of apricot jam Evelyn gave me?" As if talking to myself would give me the answer. I pushed boxes and cans around on the pantry shelves. I had too much stored food for a person living alone. "What are the light bulbs doing behind the applesauce?" Ordinarily, an organized person, I was frustrated by the disarray of the cluttered pantry. Worse, it was if I was noticing the clutter for the first time! Pasta, spaghetti... The telephone rang, interrupting my search for apricot jam.

It was Lorraine asking for Grace's cell number. I knew it wasn't on my iphone contact list. I did remember scribbling it on the back of an envelope and sticking it in my catch-all kitchen drawer. Lorraine held on while my fingers dug into the over-stuffed drawer. I pulled out old coupons, a tarnished silver salad spoon left by a mystery pot-luck guest, pointless pencils, three half-burned birthday candles and $1.44 in change. Finally, I pulled out the crumpled envelope from the back of the drawer.

After we hung up, my dormant spring cleaning instincts took over. I grabbed a few plastic grocery bags from under the sink and went to work, culling clutter from cupboards and drawers, muttering, "When in doubt, throw it out!"

The next morning, buoyed by my kitchen success, I tackled the rest of the house, room by room. How long ago had I absent-mindedly hidden peanut brittle in my winter sweater drawer?

Before I could stop and think, I opened a drawer crammed with *his* things. A shoe brush, once-used tuxedo studs, a pack of gum, a scenic postcard of London, a yellow tennis ball and finally, a long-expired roll of unopened 35 mm film. I wondered if I could sell it as a collectable on eBay?

Absorbed by my aloneness, I had put off, swept under the carpet, so to speak, and ignored the getting on with life. I had allowed clutter to congregate in more than cupboards and closets. Clutter had moved unchecked into the cubby holes of my mind.

Perhaps you are a little like me. Do you routinely leave your grocery list at home or forget to buy the item you went for? Do you send birthday cards, forgetfully addressing the envelope to your own town? Did you ever accidently use aerosol foam shower cleanser instead of hair spray? Forget to pay a utility bill on time?

Once we finally put our house in order, it's not easy to keep it that way. That takes concentration and organization. Keeping order in your home is much the same as prioritizing your life. Clutter is the result of decisions to postpone what eventually must be addressed.

Jesus tells us in Luke 10:42, to do as Mary did and set aside clutter that distracts us from opening our hearts and minds to His Word. He also warned in Matthew 12, that if our minds are swept clean but left barren, Satan will be quick to return and take up residence with his band of demons. Our safeguard is to fill our minds with things of Christ.

When we toss out the clutter found in our homes and in our minds, we gain a sense of freedom and control. Our homes then have room for us and for God's direction in our lives.

Footnote: *"Do not store up for yourselves treasures on earth, where moths and vermin destroy, and where thieves break in and steal. But store up for yourselves treasures in heaven, where moths and vermin do not destroy and where thieves do not break in and steal. For where your treasure is, there your heart will be also."* (Matthew 6:19-21)

Footprint: *Lord, furnish the rooms of my mind and heart with a passion for Your Word. Amen.*

Stress Be Gone!

Scripture Focus
PSALM 5:11
MATTHEW 5:12A

THE LOSS OF A SPOUSE is enough to catapult a woman into stress overload. Well-meaning relatives, friends and perhaps your pastor or family doctor, offer the same advice – pray, relax, take a deep breath, think about the good times, keep busy, pray. Secretly, you feel like screaming out, "I do, I can't, I try, it doesn't help, I do!"

So, what *is* helpful? Take a serious look at the following list of 95 practical ways to lower your stress level. The list was compiled by women who have walked alone in bedroom slippers worn thin in the same places as yours.

A few of the suggestions are outside your comfort zone. Try them anyway. Some are surprisingly simple. Each lightens the spirit, which lifts depression and lowers the stress level. The result is that you feel better about yourself for the moment. Moments multiply into one day at a time.

95 Ways To Lower Your Stress

Lay out your clothes and accessories the night before – throw a paper airplane – take an herbal bubble bath – meet the sunrise in Bible study – yell at a ball game – exercise to a CD – use scented bath powder – buy lacy underwear – eat breakfast by candlelight – include silverware, a cloth napkin and place mat in your lunch – keep a journal – get up 15 minutes earlier to take a 10 minute walk – memorize Psalm 121 – eat lunch with a view – tuck a $100 bill in your wallet - make duplicate keys – watch snails – fix something that's broken – ask someone "How are you?" then listen – make a list of your computer passwords – carry an umbrella in the car – say hello to a passing stranger – look at problems as opportunities – buy a china tea cup at a garage sale.

Walk through an art gallery – put up a bird feeder – have a Plan B – learn a new doodle – learn where your power, gas and water shut-offs are – do a 500 piece jigsaw puzzle – swing as high as you can on a swing set, hum a jingle – patty-cake with a toddler – bathe by moonlight – tell someone how nice he/she looks –do a zip line with a friend – remember you always have options – take a different route to church – write a letter to a far-away friend – attend your high school reunion – put air freshener in your car.

Give yourself a facial – paint your toenails – get a pap smear and mammogram – find the Big Dipper – read a poem – hold a baby – get a body massage—visualize yourself winning – walk in the rain – plant an herb garden – read a novel – hug a tree—clean out a closet—make a cake from scratch – ask someone to be your prayer partner – walk your precinct before a local election – eat popcorn and cry during a movie – listen to a symphony – teach a kid to fly a kite – avoid negative people – buy a houseplant – put safety first – send an e-card to a friend for no special occasion.

Press a flower – volunteer – update your checkbook –say "no" and don't feel guilty – stop a bad habit – set out a guest book – greet at Sunday service – take in a rescue pet – learn to whistle a tune – tell someone to have a good day in Pig Latin – browse the library stacks – research your family's roots on Ancestry.com – resist gossiping – add red bell pepper to green salad – teach a child to play jacks – subscribe to a new magazine – take dance lessons – clip coupons -- walk along the ocean or lake shore – do a crossword puzzle – join a ladies Bible study – get a dental check-up – visit an antique shop -- bake and freeze quick breads for Christmas gifts – change your hair style – buy yourself a bakery treat – wear your mother's jewelry – go to a Mary Kay make-over – buy a new nightgown -- go to a full service gas station – buy a brightly colored scarf – print your favorite Bible verse on a card and tape it to your bathroom mirror – take old books to the book exchange – try a new tea – accept God's unconditional love.

Footnote: Using your own experience as a guide, add several new stress relievers to the above list. Share the entire list with a friend. Then laugh together!

Footprint: *"Restore to me the joy of your salvation and uphold me with a willing spirit."* (Psalm 51:12)

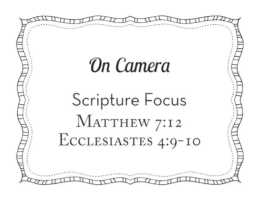

On Camera

Scripture Focus
MATTHEW 7:12
ECCLESIASTES 4:9-10

MY FRIEND, Joy, recently told me the story of a lesson she'd learned from a very wise woman.

Joy began, "I was in the front yard, watering my newly-planted birch, when I saw my neighbor coming across the street. Julia was smiling and waving a pair of tickets. I put down the hose and met her at the fence."

"The annual Boys and Girls Club Benefit is next Saturday night," Julia's eyes danced as she talked. "Smitty will be away fishing. Will you be my guest?"

"Just a second," I said, buying time as I stepped gingerly through the gazanias to turn off the water. The idea of going out socially, only to be cornered with questions like "Where's your better-half?" or trapped by the ice-breaker, "What does your husband do?" made my skin crawl.

I know you like this sort of thing," Julia went on as I retraced my steps back to her. "Between the two of us, we'll know most of the people attending."

I started to speak, but the tears welled up, choking my words. Finally, I blurted out, "Julia, I don't want to talk to anyone. Only my family and a few neighbors know Dale and I are separated and getting a divorce. I don't like any part of what's happening." Then lastly, I pinched out, "People will think the worst, that I drove 'Mr. Popularity' away."

Julie stood there, waiting for some explanation.

I meekly offered, "Your social butterfly neighbor has become what *is not* me – a wounded bird with clipped wings."

Julia crossed her arms, thoughtfully. She cleared her throat -- in preparation for a lecture, I supposed. When she spoke, it was with a softness that reached across the fence, touching the ache in my heart.

"Welcome to my side of the fence. I know the feeling well. No sense you suffering as long as I did. Are you willing to give my remedy a try? It doesn't hurt, costs nothing and you'll soon be your old, sparkling self."

I nodded cautiously, not verbally committing.

"Close enough. Come with me to the benefit. I'll show you how to draw closer to people without threatening your temporary tenderness. I can almost promise that you will give the night-out a two thumbs up! Julie tagged on, "There has to be a first step. I will help you take it. Someone helped me."

On the way to the benefit, Julie began her private tutoring with, "Let Matthew 7:12 be this evening's guide —'*Do unto others, as you would have them do unto you.*' In this case, show an interest in others. You won't have to talk about yourself."

She elaborated. "It's simple. Pretend you are a camera. Just use a few photographic tricks to use while mingling."

Focus on the subject. Ask simple questions about comfortable aspects in your subject's life. "Are you looking forward to retirement?" "How do you like grand-parenting?" "Did your roses survive the heat wave?" When you speak, continue the topic introduced by another person instead of changing the subject abruptly. People's first love is talk about themselves.

Look behind the lens. Make eye contact as you listen to him/her share in the conversation. Has he/she lost a mother, spouse or a job? Recovering from an accident or illness? Picturing another's burden helps put one's own life in perspective.

Watch the body language. Pose yourself to face the person you address. Avoid looking past the subject to the scene beyond. A firm handclasp or light touch helps develop a genuine feeling of caring.

Assure a positive exposure. Sometimes you will forget a person's name a second after hearing it. Asking to have it repeated puts you in a good light. It shows genuine interest.

Watch for photo opportunities. At every gathering, someone is standing apart. He or she probably knows fewer people than you do. Greet that person with special warmth. It's an easy shot when you share complimentary comments about the hosts, or that old stand-by – the weather.

I followed Julia's counsel. The evening went well, as she said it would. The next time I venture into a crowd scene, I'll be ready with my camera. I'm praying that It won't be long before I develop a positive image about me and my new life.

Footnote: Sometimes God shows us that grass can be greener on the other side of the fence. Take steps to look at life from another's viewpoint.

Footprint: *"I was a stranger and you invited me in."* (Matthew 25:35)

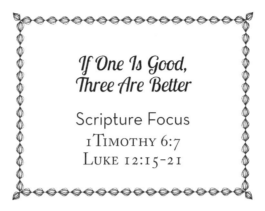

*If One Is Good,
Three Are Better*

Scripture Focus
1 TIMOTHY 6:7
LUKE 12:15-21

SADIE FINISHED her grapefruit before thumbing through the sightseeing brochures I'd left on her nightstand the evening before.

"Which is it going to be? Safari Park or a harbor excursion? I inquired of my weekend houseguest.

"How about going shopping at the new mall?" She countered.

An hour later, we were standing in Macy's shoe department. Sadie, recently widowed, was contemplating the purchase of an expensive pair of shoes. "I've not seen this brand in Seattle. Well, why not? They are beyond comfortable." Sadie turned to the clerk. "I'll take a pair in each of the three colors!"

I gasped. "Lord, help me hold my tongue," I thought. Sadie had barely enough in the bank to re-sole her old shoes.

Sadie whipped out her VISA, signed the charge slip with a smile. She turned to me, "Ready to look at earrings? I noticed a sale sign when we came in."

Keeping the average shopper as a return buyer is vital to our economic system. From Amazon to Madison Avenue, we can find all we could possibly need or desire. It's up to each of us to filter cravings from common sense purchases. Those of us who are suddenly alone are especially vulnerable. Why? Because our present lifestyle is not always of our own choosing. It hurts. We are searching for a pain-killer. More of something makes us feel safe, protected against further emptiness. We have control over something.

Our society has ready antidotes for pain. Acquisitions. Status. TV ads blare the twisted truth that ownership of "things" will make us more attractive, more loveable, happier, sexier.

Ruthann's husband died in May. Alone, she began to watch more TV. Before long, Ruthann discovered a shopping channel. Her first purchase gave her a power rush. She had control over something! The second item she purchased promised "instant glamour." Before long, she was keeping her credit card beside her on an end table. Ruthann broadened her control to include kitchen items, jewelry, figurines and clocks.

Neighbors observed a UPS truck rolling up to her front walk at least once a week. This went on for months until her daughter arrived for a visit. Natalie found her mother's guest room stacked with hundreds of boxes, most unopened.

"Why?" her daughter stammered.

"Every time I make a purchase, the program host announces 'It's Ruthann, ordering such and such. It's nice to hear from you today.' Or, 'You have made a great choice! It's our highest quality blender."

"Folks, Ruthann has ordered three days in a row. She's become part of our TV family. We love you, Ruthann.'"

Why did Ruthann fail to discipline herself, allowing her home to become a storehouse for a garage sale? She nibbled away at the edges of loneliness by basking in brief moments of recognition, appreciation and status afforded by the TV host. She found a friend in the respectful, pleasant delivery driver, who came to call her by her first name.

The key to fulfillment in our lives is refusing to allow past disappointments control us. There is no purchase that will remove pain. There is no status money can buy that will make us feel whole.

Jesus wants to comfort us in our sorrow. He is the remedy for emptiness and pain. God promises never to leave us, never to disappoint us, according to His words in Psalms 16:11 *"You have made known to me the path of life; you will fill me with joy in your presence, with eternal pleasures at your right hand."*

Is there a time for shopping? Of course. Beautiful things are God's creation, too, and have a place in our lives. Some are inherited with a precious legacy. Others are rewards for hard work and prudent living. "Things" will never bring us joy if acquired to provide us with a sense of completeness.

Before you buy, ask yourself: "Can my bank account afford this? Is it something I will actually use or wear? Would I make a special trip to the store tomorrow to buy it?"

One "NO" answer means it's time to go for a long walk in the country. Wear your old shoes!

Footnote: Buy only what is on your shopping list today. Postpone the purchase of impulse items until tomorrow. For some things, tomorrow never comes.

Footprint: *"It is better to take refuge in the Lord than to trust in man. It is better to take refuge in the Lord than to trust in princes."* (Psalm 118: 8- 9)

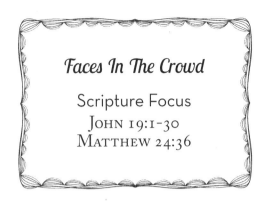

Faces In The Crowd

Scripture Focus
JOHN 19:1-30
MATTHEW 24:36

WE HOLD SOUP SUPPERS in the church's parish hall before Lenten services on Wednesday nights. One evening, I decided not to go to the supper. Although I dislike eating alone, the thought of walking in on a crowd of happy families breaking bread together suddenly made me feel as alone as the day my world turned upside down.

I slow-poked, arriving for the church service a few minutes late. I slipped unnoticed into one of the few empty seats. I had no time to "crowd panic." I was immediately captivated by the drama of the Passion story unfolding from the pulpit.

Pastor asked us to focus our thoughts on the faces in the crowd at the foot of Calvary. We were to contemplate how, within a short week in history, each of lives of the principle cast members was changed forever.

Only a few days before the gruesome scene at Golgotha, Mary listened with a full heart as multitudes waved palm fronds and shouted of her firstborn, "Hosanna to the Son of David." Then, still within that same week, the same citizens demanded, "Crucify Him!" His broken body hung limp on the cross above her.

John supped and prayed with Jesus that last evening as they shared the Passover feast in the upper room. Grief stricken and still within that short week, John would mourn the tortured death of his dear friend at the foot of the bloody cross.

Pilate, frustrated with his assignment, condemned the Son of God to death. Peter, the Rock, despaired of the guilt and shame of denial as the cock crowed three times. Judas, the betrayer for thirty pieces of silver, died by his own hand, as he swung from a tree.

Everyone makes the choice to accept or reject Calvary's cross. Only God knows the day and the hour *"It is finished,"* for each of us.

Gratefully, Lord, I lay the burden of all my lonely hours at the foot of Calvary and turn my face toward the victory of the cross! I am no longer alone in that Good Friday crowd.

Where do you stand in the crowd?

Footnote: When was the last time you had the opportunity to speak out for Christ? Did you face Calvary or did you turn away?

Footprint: *"So shall our song of triumph ever be: Praise to the Crucified for victory! Lift high the cross,* *the loved of Christ proclaim, Till all the world adore His sacred name."*

"Lift High The Cross"
George Kitchen/Michael R. Newbold

Skyjacked!

Scripture Focus
JAMES 1:2-4
ROMANS 8:28

THE REVEREND JOHN SWARTZ sat across from me at the glass-topped table on my sundeck. He shared the story of his flight from Dallas to San Diego by way of Cuba.

In retrospect, skyjacking was probably the first "terrorist" act upon the ordinary U.S. citizen. At that time, in the sixties, individually, and as a nation, we abhorred the increasing number of random attacks on private citizens in peaceful nations. We no longer felt completely safe. There was no way we could have imagined the evil that lurked in the years to come.

John Swartz recalled his adventure in a richly-toned monologue. "We were at 35,000 feet, high above Texas, homing in on Communist Cuba at 600 miles an hour. The pilot was guided by a nickel-plated pistol. Even so, I knew God was not making a mistake. I know the truth in Romans 8, *'that in everything God works for good with those who love Him, who are called according to His purpose.'*"

John talked of a quiet that pervaded the passenger cabin, as each fought the storm of human fears with his own prayers.

I whispered, daringly, "What did you learn from that soul-wrenching day?"

He pondered for a moment, looked east toward the hills that cupped our little valley, seemingly searching for the right words.

His voice was a soft as my whispered question. "God allowed me the awesome privilege to learn first-hand what He tells us in James 1:2, *Count it all joy, my brethren, when you meet various trials, for you know that testing of your faith produces steadfastness.*"

Somewhere in his race across the dark heavens, Pastor Swartz had touched the hem of God's wisdom. His expression, as he spoke, radiated an inner peace that passed my own understanding, until I experienced my own night-sky drama.

I had flown in my friend's Cesena Turbo 210 many times over the years. Even though Bob was an excellent pilot, it took me plenty of prayer time to feel comfortable suspended in the air in a tomato soup-can-thin tube. Commercial airliners, with slightly thicker skin, do not reduce my pre-board anxiety.

We'd had a good trip, flying 150 miles north to visit my new granddaughter. I was relaxed on our return flight, the vibration of the engine lulling me into mental reminiscing.

Over the years, how many square miles of God's creation had I been privileged to view from this birds eye vantage point? I was counting the past destination points when the plane began its descent into the Ramona Airport landing pattern. The tiny runway below shown like a welcoming yellow ribbon in the moonlight.

Bob reached to cycle the landing gear. It refused to lower! We were in trouble!

We circled the dark, rural airfield again and again, always banking left as Bob tried to cycle the gear. Bob remained calm. I prayed for a Jacob's ladder!

An hour later, we were still cutting holes in the sky. Bob tried every known standard emergency procedure, including several suggestions from his airplane mechanic, who had been contacted by Ontario Approach.

Finally, Bob leveled the Cessna, setting a heading north to Riverside Airport, where fire trucks, foam and his mechanic awaited our landing. Flight authorities asked for the telephone numbers or our next of kin. I imagined curious on-lookers lining the field, kids on bicycles selling popcorn. Silliness invaded my monster nightmare.

Then abruptly, I heard Jesus speak to me as clearly as he had to John Swartz. I heard, "*Count it all joy....when you meet various trials, testing of your faith ....all good for those who love Him.*"

I knew that God was talking to me personally. I did not know the ending to our crisis, but He knew. I let go, giving God control over me, realizing He'd always had control over our situation. I finally understood how John Swartz' could sense inner peace in the midst of a life and death situation.

As we neared Riverside, flight control advised us that we were in the flight path of an incoming 747 to LAX. Bob banked right, as told, and once again, tried to cycle the gear.

The gear-down light turned green! The growling gear lowered! Within minutes, we were safely on terra firma.

Later, we learned that we'd lost all but a few drops of hydraulic fluid in the gear reservoir. When the plane banked right, the pick-up tube, located in the right bottom corner, sucked up those last drops, building enough pressure to cycle the gear one more time.

I have always feared flying, anticipating the worst because I had no control over my destiny. When I had to face my worst nightmare, I discovered that I, alone, could do nothing. When I made the choice to trust my life into His keeping, I experienced the awesome gift of perfect inner peace!

Footnote: Don't spend another worrisome moment. Give God your fears. Know His peace. *"So don't worry about tomorrow: for tomorrow will* *worry about itself. Each day has enough trouble of its own.* (Matthew 6:24)

Footprint: *God of all the Heavens above, who sent His only Son to give His life so that we may have life eternal, thank you for skyjacking me, teaching me that I am never alone in the hour of trial. Keep me in that heavenly state of inner peace. Amen.*

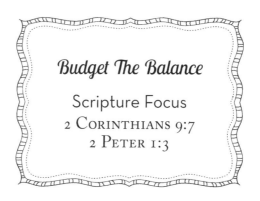

Budget The Balance

Scripture Focus
2 CORINTHIANS 9:7
2 PETER 1:3

BECKY STOOD a few people ahead of me in the teller line. We had first met at a meeting of Heart Healers, a local church's reach-out ministry for those who are grieving.

I was surprised to find her waiting when I finished my bank business some minutes later. "Visiting the main branch? Doesn't everyone living across the bridge bank by mail?" I teased.

She laughed. "Usually. I had some stuff to do that can only be done at the main office. I'm glad that our paths crossed. I've been meaning to call you. Do you have a couple of minutes?"

We moved to a quiet corner in the lobby, settling ourselves on the bank's sofa, near the coffee bar. Becky explained why it was me, in particular, she wanted to contact. She was now like me – alone.

"How do I decide how much to give to God? Do I give a percentage based on gross or net income? What's the difference between an offering and a tithe?"

I thought a moment and replied, "God loves a cheerful giver. You get that. Let's tackle the rest of your question." I then told Becky, trying not to sound preachy, "The Bible teaches the principle of tithing ten per cent. That much belongs to God." (Numbers 18:26 and Matthew 23:23).

"Offerings," I continued, "provide us with the opportunity to thank God for everything He gives us. A free-will offering should be added to one's tithe."

Becky zeroed in on what soon emerges as a major concern for those of us learning to live alone. "My husband gave our tithe based on gross or net income, I don't know which. Either way, I'm not certain I can match the percentage. My income is lower now, but my mortgage and taxes remain the same."

Her concerns were my concerns not long ago. It was my own Pastor Jim, who put my mind at ease. He reminded me that giving is not a matter of money alone, but of attitude. He pointed out four basic truths found in God's Word.

What I have, God owns. "For everything in heaven and earth is yours. Yours, O Lord." (I Chronicles 29:11b). When I work from that mind-set, it's easier to be generous.

What I need, God supplies. *"My God shall supply all your needs according to his riches in glory."* (Philippians 4:19). He cares for the birds in the fields, the lilies in the valley and for me every single day. He is faithful to His promise. You and I are richly blessed to have a roof over our heads and food on the table every day.

What I give, God will multiply. *"Now he who supplies seed to the sower and bread for food will also supply and increase your store of seed and will enlarge the harvest of your righteousness."*

(2 Corinthians 9:10)

Give generously and watch for tenfold blessing in return, my Pastor assured me. I tried it once on a small scale. It worked. I've come to enjoy reaching out, giving. The ten-fold blessing is always returned, often in different ways, as promised. A bonus: We all know the inner joy that comes from giving over receiving.

What I invest, God rewards. *"For everyone who has, will be given more, and he will have an abundance."* (Matthew 25:29). God rewards those who invest their time, talents, and treasures in His kingdom. Too often, we are busy gaining things for ourselves. We miss the best God has to offer.

I was beginning to sound like a college lecturer. Becky was lost, mired in too much information, too fast. She'd wanted the "Tithing for Dummies," version.

"Becky," I concluded, "The way to give to God is to follow Paul's advice in 1 Corinthians 16:2. '*On the first day of the every week, each one of you should set aside a sum of money in keeping with his income.*' I store my church envelopes with my mortgage coupons. I write both checks at the same time."

It works for me.

Footnote: Pray for guidance with your checkbook open! Give to God first, then budget the balance. Faithfulness in giving will actually help you balance your budget.

Footprint: *"We give thee but Thine own, Whate're the gift may be; All that we have is Thine alone, A trust, O Lord, from Thee."*

"We Give Thee But Thine Own"
William W. How, 1854

A Fish Tale

Scripture Focus
GENESIS 1:20-25
MATTHEW 21:22

I STOOD ON THE FLYING BRIDGE and let the salt air whip through my hair, as we skimmed across the southern tip of Alaska's Inside Passage, heading for Ship Island and, hopefully, schools of silver salmon.

It was hard for me to comprehend that I'd had breakfast in my own kitchen this morning in Southern California, and now, at lunchtime, I was watching a bald eagle soar above Ketchikan's magnificent shoreline.

The dream began when I was little girl, trolling the kelp beds off La Jolla shores in my dad's English dory. I believed my father's fish tales, and prayed that one day, I, too, could fish for Alaskan salmon in the frigid waters of America's Last Frontier.

Life happens. Marriage. Children. A bigger home. Before I could share my dream adventure with my husband, our time together was over. I was alone, still adventurism in my heart.

One day, unexpectedly, one of my friends called. He was putting together an Alaskan fishing party for interested couples, singles, and families. My dream came alive. My childhood hope realized.

Now, standing high above the water, I watched the eagle swoop down to the water and snatch a salmon in its talons. A half-grown bear wrestled a mossy log on the beach along the distant shore. A few minutes later, I spotted two hump back whales blowing across our wake as they migrated southward.

I gripped the chrome railing, the sea air flying in my face. I sensed God beside me. He was looking through my eyes with me as I tried to etch in my forever-memory His multi-dimensional creation that stretched from horizon to horizon. I saw myself, a dream-filled child, at the center of His vast diorama. God was sharing the fulfillment of my dream with me. I was not alone and I knew it!

As surely as the salmon is driven to return to its particular spawning grounds on an exact timetable, as surely as the whale turns southward on the long journey to deliver its young in warmer waters and as God promises to care for the birds and lilies of the field, so also does our Heavenly Father provide for our needs and our desires according to His time. Today's abundant joy is often yesterday's answered prayer.

Footnote: The wonder of God's creation is everywhere – in our own backyards, in our own dioramas. Enjoy nature's seasonal timing. Hang a bird feeder and bird house outside in view of your kitchen window.

Footprint: *"Beautiful Savior, King of Creation, Son of God and Son of Man! Truly I'd love Thee, Truly I'd serve Thee, Light of my soul, my Joy, my Crown."*

"Fair are the meadows, Fair are the woodlands, Robed in flowers of blooming spring; Jesus is fairer, Jesus is purer; He makes our sorrowing spirit sing."

"Beautiful Savior"
Author Unknown 1677

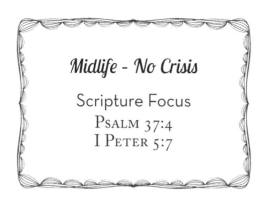

Midlife - No Crisis

Scripture Focus
PSALM 37:4
I PETER 5:7

MEGAN CALLED IT "chewing on dragons."
She tells us her story in her own words.

Chewing on dragons – when every fantasy became, in my mind, a living nightmare. A cutting remark pierced so deeply that I felt my heart contract in pain. When I reached out to another and met a distracted glance, rejection flooded me with the force of a tidal wave. I was 45 years old and felt fine physically, but emotionally, the dragons of pain and rejection waited to overwhelm me.

I prayed. The march of raging warriors strode through the dark passages of my imagination. My bubbly nature shriveled, until it searched for a crevice where I could hide. I prayed some more.

It was time for my annual PAP smear. I had time to think and pray as I stared at the ceiling, waiting for my doctor to come in. I didn't doubt God, I doubted myself. Was I praying for the wrong thing, praying selfishly?

Finally, it was my turn. I heard him outside my door. Dr. Shaw stepped in and with a broad smile, asked, "How are you feeling?"

"Fine," I managed cheerily. Then, the tears welled up and the pent-up tidal wave of secret pain spilled out. As I blubbered, I was certain Dr. Shaw thought I was ready for the funny farm.

Surprisingly, he took my hand and said, "I believe tests will show you have an hormone deficiency. Not uncommon at your age. I'm going to give you some help."

One painless injection and 30 minutes later, my body was awash with a rose-colored feeling of peace. My emotional balance improved measurably with monthly injections over the next several months. I became an evangelist for Hormone Replacement Therapy – HRT.

I learned to accept my symptoms of menopause, including depression, as normal and to trust that I would overcome. Victory would come sooner if I helped myself.

The first step was to allow myself the sense of satisfaction in any task accomplished, from cleaning one room completely, to organizing a photo album. I watched my diet, concentrating on simple meals of fresh, natural foods eaten at regular intervals. I learned to enjoy the crunch of leafy, green vegetables.

I discovered a rich sense of well-being by taking long daily walks. I found so much to see, from patterns in lawn-cutting to unusual mail boxes.

Many women as early as age thirty-five suffer menopausal symptoms such as irritability, anxiety, hot flashes and/or night sweats. Some suffer vaginal dryness, urinary problems, insomnia, and that dragon – depression.

Crisis, most specifically, the loss of a spouse, for whatever reason, can send a woman's biological speedometer into a racing gear. It happens, more often than not.

If you are suddenly alone and/or are under 100 years old and feel a little out-of-sync physically or emotionally, quit drag'in. Call for an appointment with your primary doctor or GYN. Be good to yourself. You are one of God's unique creations. You deserve the best! Claim victory over your dragons!

Footnote: Ask your doctor about E.R.T. or vitamin E as a substitute. Maybe all you need to feel victorious is a pill or a patch. Follow through. Do what your doctor advises to slay your dragons!

Footprint: *"Then He said to her, "Daughter, your faith has healed you. Go in peace."* (Luke 8:48)

The Forever Stamp

Scripture Focus
GENESIS 1:27
ISAIAH 64:8

REMEMBER WHEN a first-class postage stamp cost three cents and everyone knew what a penny post card was? Remember, too, when "neither snow, nor rain, nor heat, nor gloom of night" kept our mailman from delivering mail to the front door twice a day?

I became enamored, as a child, with our rural-style mailbox the first time I found something in it addressed to me, personally. It was an introductory issue of *Jack and Jill* magazine.

The first letter I received was postmarked from Del Mar, California, addressed in a pre-teen scrawl by Sydney, a soul-sister I met at Girl Scout camp the month before. I excitedly replied the next day. That was the last time either of us wrote.

It wasn't long before graduation party invitations, notes from friends away at college or in the service trickled into our mailbox. I remember the first elegantly addressed white wedding invitation that included my name on the inner envelope. And finally, gloriously, my own mailbox, brimming with Christmas cards addressed to Mr. and Mrs.

The cost of postage has multiplied many times since I opened Sydney's written pledge of undying friendship. The rise of social media has not totally shut down personal communication. The mailman still brings assorted bills, renewal notices, solar energy ads, a few political fund-raising invitations and fewer and fewer Christmas cards.

I don't need to read over your shoulder to know that most of the mail deposited in your mailbox is still addressed to hubby and the little Mrs.

By now, our family and friends know that we are alone. We know we are alone. It's the "forever stamp" that we are not ready to address, even though the bond is broken. Could it be, that:

— We see ourselves as unattached halves, unwilling to get on with the task of seeking our own identities and developing ourselves as complete persons?

— We believe that our culture in general, our church family in particular, subconsciously judges women alone as having less to offer intellectually, financially and emotionally than those living under the umbrella of a husband?

— We lack the faith to believe that we may still experience a rewarding life through close friendships, professional dedication, educational growth and spiritual outreach?

— We resist publically acknowledging our state of aloneness because we don't like the "broken forever" that we assume others can read stamped on our foreheads?

Whatever the excuse, you and I know there is no forever with anyone, any time or any place on this earth. Our "forever" was stamped in Christ's blood on Calvary. It's time for us to deliver ourselves into Christ's care. It's time to let go and address the uniqueness that is ours until Christ returns to carry us to our forever home.

Footnote: Let's pledge to fill out the change-of-name cards and mail them this week!

Footprint: *Heavenly Father, Comforter, Master Designer, Teacher, Savior, Redeemer -- addressed by any name, You are the potter, I am the clay. Mold me, Lord, into my birthright of wholeness, peace and communion beside You, forever. Amen*

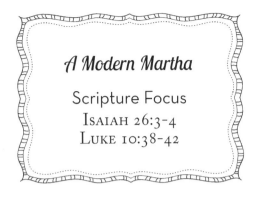

A Modern Martha

Scripture Focus
ISAIAH 26:3-4
LUKE 10:38-42

I SHIFTED RESTLESSLY in my hospital bed like a caged animal. I was shocked when the doctor quietly put away his stethoscope, closed his notebook and prepared to leave without more than a "See you in awhile."

He hadn't told me what I was to do with my time, while I waited on his return. My Kindle, my i Phone and even my knitting, were all left at home.

Sensing my agitation, he smiled kindly, patted my hand and said, "Unwind. Take deep breaths and pray. Take a nap, Martha."

Before I could protest that I hadn't taken a nap in my adult life, he was gone and I found myself complaining to a closed door.

What to do, what to do? I felt like the white rabbit in *Alice in Wonderland,* beginning the longest day of my life. I wasn't deathly ill, just miserably so, with something akin to "burn-out." I wasn't sick enough to forget I had responsibilities and that I was neglecting my busy schedule.

Soon, I found myself stretched out and looking up. Words like adversity, character, wait and patience slipped into my mind.

A picture of distant peace took shape on the ceiling above. I reached out in prayer to call it closer.

Dr. Allerton had called me Martha. My name isn't Martha, or is it? Still tightly wound, I opened the bedside drawer and pulled out the Gideon Bible. I found Martha's story in St. Luke. I found myself as well. The question is, did I find you, too?

Martha "was cumbered about much serving," and wanted her sister, Mary, to help. Jesus admonished Martha, saying of the woman sitting attentively at His feet, "*Mary hath chosen the good part, which shall not be taken away from her.*"

The world has benefited greatly from Marthas. Most heroines of science, the arts and politics have been Marthas. Marthas tackle commitments zealously and tirelessly. They find time to tackle still one more challenge.

We Marthas, who are alone, are rarely "out of service." More than once, I've been awakened after midnight by a telephone caller saying, "I know it's late to call, but as you have no husband to disturb…" I have also said "yes" to requests that begin with, "Now that you are alone and have more free time, I need…"

In truth, I have twice the chores and half the help. The fact that I am needed by someone, fuels my spirit.

Unfortunately, today's society places a higher value on speed rather than contentment. We Marthas tend to gear up at 6 am, move out into the fast lane and never let up on the gas. God knew I was on a collision course. He wisely pulled me in for a pit stop. Should you have your breaking ability checked, too?

Taking a deep breath, relaxing and pushing a tight schedule to the sideline is hard medicine for a Martha to swallow. When a Martha guns it back on the highway, proper maintenance means learning to say "no" when the speedometer starts to climb. For a Martha, safe driving is slower driving, slow enough to smell the roses along the way. That *is* the challenge for a Martha.

Footnote: List three times in the last month you should have said "no" without apology. Try to carve out three days during the next week when you can begin the day with a fifteen-minute quiet time with Jesus. Do you need to rethink your driving pattern?

Footprint: *Lord, teach me to monitor my schedule to include a quiet time with Your Word. Incline my ears to listen with the care and patience of a Mary, that I may not only love to live, but take time to live to love. Amen.*

It Takes Two

Scripture Focus
1 JOHN 3:18
1 JOHN 4:7

"How ARE YOU?" she asked, passing by me in the produce aisle of our local super market.

She and her cart hurried on. She was stopped at the lettuce display by the time I was able to respond with a wilted, "Fine." She didn't hear me. She was focused on selecting the best head. I felt a pinprick of rejection. I wish we'd not met up at all. I continued on my way to the meat counter.

I meet such women quite often and not always in the grocery store. Sometimes, our paths cross at the post office, in the mall or sadly, on the steps after church. The scenario is "ditto" of the above. What a dehumanizing exchange! Even worse, I realized that I am often guilty of the same pointless exercise.

One of the virtues I have come to appreciate, since I've been single again, is sincerity in others. However, when I look for it in others I am often disappointed. When I am inwardly sincere and outwardly open, I mirror the likeness of the caring person God intends me to be. My inner spirit is nurtured.

Following are the four "T's" that cast the warmth of Christian caring over every greeting.

Talk: We met at the photo center at Costco. When Irene replied "Fine," I did not move away. She continued, "I've just returned from Elk Meadows. I learned to ski!" she beamed.

I looked at my stocky, fifty-five year-old friend. A wisp of grey hair hung down over one eye. Had I rushed off, I would have missed the sharing of this historic moment in her life. "I am so proud of you!" My tone reflected honest admiration for her accomplishment. Irene felt welcomed in another's life for the moment. I felt richer, learning of her courage.

Touch: As a transition from a double to single lifestyle, I find that I need a few extra squeezes and hugs to replace the ones no longer available to me.

My friend, Judy, gives the best hugs. I feel God's love energizing me when Judy's arms are wrapped around me, even for a second or two. I'm glad she reaches out. The other day, I told her how much her hugs mean to me. She was speechless for a moment by my honest confession. I'm trying to learn to be as open as Judy, in sharing God's love from my heart to another's, with a touch on the shoulder, a squeeze or sometimes in an all-out hug. Some touches are shared in joy, some in empathy and some in sympathy. I've discovered even the lightest touch is rewarding for both of us.

Tears: Tears are the spillway of the heart. Karen couldn't hold them back when confiding that her daughter asked her not to come for the birth of her first baby, since the other grandmother was closer. I cried with her. We both felt better and our friendship was strengthened through caring and sharing.

Time: It is what I had little of, when I stopped by Caroline's to deliver freshly-cut autumn roses from my garden. She had been immobilized with severe back pain. As I took steps to leave, I noticed a pleading in her eyes. I mentally canceled my next errand, smiled, and suggested I arrange the flowers while we chatted.

Caroline told me that her husband needed immediate surgery. Her back responded to the unexpected stress with waves of excruciating pain. She needed to make several arrangements by phone. Could I take time to wait while she called her son? He could arrive soon and take over. Could we pray together first?

"Of course," I replied sincerely, feeling the closeness of God's eternal friendship.

My two teen-age granddaughters gave me a car license plate frame for my birthday that reads, "God Loves You, But I Am His Favorite." You have the same frame around you. Wear it proudly.

Footnote: List a concern troubling you. List a joy ready for sharing. Call a friend. Ask, "How are you?" Leap beyond the robotic response. Listen in love, share with sincerity. Know that you are His favorite!

Footprint: Someone who loves you is watching. Visit Him daily in prayer. Include your friends' concerns among your petitions and their friendships among your praises.

Lost And Found

Scripture Focus
PSALM 66:16
LUKE 15:8-10

I SEARCHED EVERYWHERE this morning for my misplaced reading glasses – on the floor beside my bed, in the trash compactor, between the couch cushions and in the laundry basket. It's very frustrating because I misplace "my eyes" at least once a week. If the host on *Family Feud* ever asks, "What is the most commonly lost item in the home?" it would have to be glasses – probably my glasses.

Second on my lost list are keys. I lose them within the folds of my purse among my wallet, compact, grocery list, checkbook, package of travel tissues and small notebook. Keys seem to take forever to find.

Sometimes *I* feel lost. It was especially true when I found myself suddenly single again, without my husband's trained eyes to help me search.

One day, while desperately hunting for my glasses, I prayed aloud, "Okay, God, You know where my glasses are hiding. Please, You find them. I have fifteen minutes to get ready for work." With that, I stopped searching and hurried to dress.

I few minutes later, I reached down to wipe a spill off the kitchen floor and spied my glasses resting on the seat of a kitchen chair! From then on, I've trusted God, who is All-Seeing, All-Knowing, to be my professional search partner. Try it. It works!

God has dealt patiently with the lost since the beginning of time. When Adam and Eve lost "Paradise on Earth," God offered Man a way to find Eternal Life. God saved Noah and his family from the Flood so that His Word would not be lost in a fallen world.

God searches after lost sheep until He finds them. Our Heavenly Father rejoices when a lost and condemned sinner repents, and accepts the free gift of Salvation by trusting in His Son, Jesus Christ, as his or her personal Savior.

I declare my wallet lost when I cannot find it. God counts it lost when I do not use its contents to serve Him. Sometimes I get laryngitis. God says my voice is lost when I do not use it in prayer and praise to Him. Time is lost when I let pass an opportunity to share the Gospel of Good News with a "lost" friend or acquaintance.

Each time I lose my glasses, I am humbly reminded of my imperfect body and poor memory. I live for the day when, at Heaven's gates, I will be fitted with a new, perfect mind and body through

Jesus' promise to remember me to His Father in Heaven.

Footnote: Is there anything you can't find? Ask God to lead you to it. Invite Him to walk beside you each day and guide your eyes along His path.

Footprint: *Thank you, Lord Jesus, for finding me, a lost sheep. Keep me close beside You as daily, I seek a deeper understanding of Your Word. Amen.*

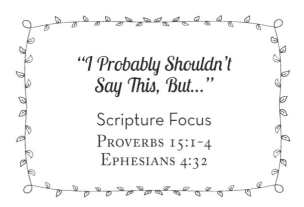

"I Probably Shouldn't Say This, But..."

Scripture Focus
PROVERBS 15:1-4
EPHESIANS 4:32

I WAS STANDING at the kitchen sink scrubbing vegetables when the phone rang. The caller was Louise.

"Do you have a minute?" she asked, then rushed on. "I refigured my week's paycheck. Kay made a sizeable error on the net amount."

"Bring it to her attention so she can correct the mistake," I suggested -- an obvious solution in my mind.

"I will, Monday. This is Friday night. I can't deposit an incorrectly figured check and I can't wait until Monday to buy groceries."

I was about to offer her grocery money when Louise snapped, "I probably shouldn't say this but Kay has a mean streak. I had to put her in her place last week. I bet she shorted my check on purpose!"

I was disappointed to hear gossip about Kay's character. "I thought Kay was your friend. She may have hurt feelings because you 'put her in her place.'"

Louise abruptly ended our conversation.

A short time later, before the vegetables finished cooking, Louise called again. Clearly, she was steaming!

"I didn't call you a few minutes ago to have you stick up for Kay. I probably shouldn't say this, but I expect that you will pass on our conversation, which will put me in a bad light. Everyone knows you embellish everything you say!" She slammed down the receiver.

My whole body felt assaulted. A tingle gained force in my head. I turned off the burner under the vegetables and buried my head in my hands. I prayed, "Lord, I'm under attack. How do I defend my character? How do I respond to Louise?" I seem to talk to God more often now that I'm alone. One of my wiser decisions, I've discovered.

His answer was immediate, faster than asking Internet Siri.

"Wait on me." God himself advised. I paused to praise His name, then ate my vegetables.

The following morning, I woke up remembering the simple, effective checklist I had saved following a recent leadership conference. I dug it out of my filing cabinet.

• Remember, "To err is human." Be prepared to be criticized when you least expect it. It will help soften the sting.

- Consider the source. Did your critic approach you in Christian love in a non-judgmental way? If so, listen in love. Did the person speak in the heat of anger? Is the person an endless fault-finder? If so, perhaps this critic has her own problem.
- Cool the confrontation. Following criticism, hurt or anger may keep you from thinking clearly. Simply say, "I realize you are trying to help. I need time to give your comments serious attention."
- Have you heard a similar criticism before? If the criticism is fairly-placed, disarm your critic by saying, "I'm sorry. Others have told me the same thing. I will try harder to work on it." Then do it.
- Defend yourself. Do not sidestep if the criticism is unjustified. When you disagree, be diplomatic. Reply with words like, "I am certain your comments are well-intended. However, I cannot agree with you."

I set aside the list and prayed. Then I dialed Louise's number. She answered quickly with an apology. Her husband had forgotten their anniversary. She wanted to "take it out on somebody." Then she added, "I probably shouldn't say this, but…"

"Then please don't!"

Footnote: Do you still smart from a recent criticism? Use the above checklist as a pathway to peace.

Footprint: *Heavenly Protector, send angels to shield me from the cutting edge of criticism. Protect me from those who criticize for selfish gain. Open my heart to words prayerfully offered to guide my spiritual growth. Amen.*

The Lady Is A Tiger!

Scripture Focus
MATTHEW 15:11
EPHESIANS 4:29

REMEMBER THE CONFLICT in Frank Stockton's *"The Lady or the Tiger?"* Something happened to remind me of the anguish the condemned prisoner felt, as he stood alone in the arena in front of two identical doors.

Behind one door paced a hungry tiger, "the fiercest and cruelest that could be procured," wrote the author. It was a beast ready to tear the prisoner to bits should he choose to open that door.

Behind the other door waited the most beautiful maiden in the land. Should the prisoner open the door behind which she stood, his innocence would be affirmed. Immediately, the lady would become his bride. Presumably, the couple would live happily ever after.

The plot thickened before the question was posed to the reader: "Which door will he choose?"

I found myself in a similar arena the evening I attended a political party fundraiser. Among the guests was Jodi McDaniel, running in an important, hotly-contested county race.

I had hoped to meet Ms. McDaniel and listen to her solutions on issues confronting the voters in our district. Her background and qualifications indicated that she would be a good fit for the job.

Her campaign flyer called her a "dedicated Christian." Single, Jodi had "acted on a calling" to run for public office.

Her opposition, the incumbent, was a "good old boy," running on a platform riddled with self-serving arrogance that had helped to cripple the local economy. A change was definitely needed!

Ms. McDaniel and I became acquainted over cheese and crackers at the refreshment table. She was delighted to have an audience with a potential supporter.

She began with, "That (expletive deleted) fool I'm running against doesn't know his — from a hole in the ground. It shouldn't be too difficult to whip his —, if we can get out the Christian vote."

I gulped, about to choke on cucumber and brie!

She was on a roll. "The other side believes that because I am a woman, I am a (expletive deleted) wimp! We'll show 'em, won't we!"

We?

The candidate continued, piercing her platform position with profanity and vulgarity. The moment someone stepped up to the table, I excused myself and moved out of earshot range.

I was offended by the trash talk sprinkled with obscenities. I was most distressed that a "Christian" woman was comfortable putting down Christ, thinking it would give her an edge competing in largely a man's world!

Sometimes, we don't realize how much of our character we expose by the language we use. People evaluate us by our ability to communicate our interests, political stand, cultural values and especially, our spiritual commitment, by the words we use and the way in which we use them.

When we misuse God's name, including pushing it with derivatives "Golly," "Holy G", or "Darn him," we misuse He who named us. If we say we don't mean anything by taking God's name in vain, we are really saying that God doesn't mean anything to us, or at the very least, our commitment to Christ is shallow. How many times could we misuse a friend's name and keep a relationship of mutual respect?

I left the fundraiser perplexed. Like the prisoner in the arena, I had only two choices. Unlike him, neither choice would make my dreams come true. On Election Day, I would be forced to cast my ballot. Which would be your choice? Why?

Footnote: Make a list of the words you use which spoil your Christian witness. Shred the list. A good rule to keep concerning the Third Commandment is to use God's name only when speaking to Him or about Him.

Footprint: "... *Take my lips and let them be, filled with messages from Thee.*"

"Take My Life and Let It Be"
Frances R. Havergal, 1874

An Hour In The Garden

Scripture Focus
GENESIS 2:8-9
PHILIPPIANS 2:9-11

MY FRIEND, Pat, tells her story:

Dr. Johnson wrote out a prescription and handed it to me across the desk. His signature was a scrawl but his orders were written clearly. *One hour's gardening on knees three times a week.*

I looked up, questioningly, "Isn't there a pill you can prescribe?"

"Broken hearts are best mended by God, not by drugs," he replied. His soft smile was framed by a crown of snow-white hair.

"What does God have to do with gardening?" I asked.

He leaned back in his squeaky chair, glanced out at the manicured landscape in front of the clinic. "Something miraculous happens when we get down on our prayer bones and dig into His earth with our hands."

"Does pruning tree roses count?" I asked, only half teasing.

"One must crawl before she walks." He patted my hand and added, "Grass roots gardening is stress prevention -- therapy none of us should outgrow. Pun intended."

The following Saturday afternoon, I began taking my medicine by digging out tenacious tendrils of deeply-rooted devil grass along the sidewalk. I planted sturdy Gerbera daisies. Behind them I set a halo of irises with a backdrop of larkspur reaching heavenward.

While digging, I unearthed a sub-culture of worms, bugs and a spider wandering in my space. I became so absorbed in the complex underworld sifting through my fingers, I almost missed the old desert tortoise ambling through my garden gate.

My garden has become a sanctuary where, as Wordsworth wrote, "...*the heavy and weary weight, Of all this unintelligible world, Is lightened.*" It is a place of solitude where I dig my rain-rusted trowel into a problem, turn it over and let it aerate. I uproot frustrations along with choke weeds, find a balance between the strong and the weak, nurture tender beginnings and learn anew to appreciate old faithfuls.

I have come to realize over-feeding and over-watering can be as deadly as neglect. No matter how I try, unforeseen forces often destroy a day's toil and like locusts, eat away at my loving efforts. Who promised me a rose garden, anyway?

Even so, my garden draws strength from heaven-sent rain and sunshine. It brings forth beauty according to its own season, setting a wise example for me.

"How does a meadow flower unfold?
Because the lovely little flower is free
Down to its root, and, in that freedom, bold"

William Wordsworth, 1770-1850

Footnote: Dig deep into the soil. A plot of land, an outdoor window box or a kitchen windowsill greenhouse – may your garden reap peace and perspective in a heartbroken world.

"For how can one draw near to God
Who has not known the feel of sod?"

June Masters Bacher

Footprint: *Creator of all that we survey – We know that the gates of the Garden of Eden are closed to the eyes of a sinful, self-centered world. Keep us mindful that freedom is rooted in the higher ground of heaven. Give me the courage to invite others into my garden, where the power of Jesus Christ Savior King, dwells within. Amen.*

A Friend In Need

Scripture Focus
PSALMS 55:22
LUKE 6:31

FOR YEARS, I enjoyed driving past the Cer-
ringtons' on my way home from work. The drapes
were usually drawn back to reveal a bay window
that glistened like a sheet of clear cellophane.
Mary Ann's "signature" was a bouquet of gar-
den-grown, brilliantly-hued flowers centered in
the picture-frame front window. She arranged
her garden pick, in what I was told, was a cloisonne' vase sent from China by her missionary
aunt a long time ago.

Mary Ann's white-cottage world came apart
two years ago last May. Her friends thought she
was coping well with the sudden loss of her husband and resulting loneliness. She gave no sign of
need because she didn't infringe upon their time
or space.

I sensed differently when I noticed her drapes
open less frequently in the late afternoons. Finally, they remained closed. Profuse blooms in her
well-tended garden became brown sticks gone to

seed. I was certain the cloisonne' vase stood empty in the closed house.

Then one day, I met Mary Ann's friend, Vivian, at the dry cleaners. "I don't know Mary Ann well enough to knock on her door," I told her. "Please check on her. Something is very much the matter."

"The last time I called her, Vivian quipped, "she insulted me and hung up. If I didn't know better, I'd say she was drunk!"

"Maybe she was." As I spoke, I wondered.

Vivian looked at me seriously, then whispered, "Do you think? I better go visit. Pray she doesn't slam the door in my face."

Fortunately, Mary Ann's friend reached out in love in time. Vivian waited patiently while an inebriated Mary Ann lashed out at her, upbraiding Vivian for prying into her life. Vivian did not expect what happened next. Mary Ann snatched up the cloisonne' vase and threw it at the brick fireplace, smashing it in a million pieces. Then, Mary Ann fell sobbing onto the sofa.

Vivian dropped down next to Mary Ann and opened her arms. She held her emotionally spent friend close until Mary Ann cried her last tear. When Vivian offered to take her friend to her doctor, Mary Ann slowly nodded in agreement.

Teetotaler Mary Ann had become a classic "late-onset" alcoholic. She is in a group that comprises one-third of all drinkers over sixty. Her alcohol dependence was triggered by the traumatic loss of her husband. Deterioration had been rapid, progressing in two years at a rate seen in alcoholics who have been drinking for twenty years.

Too often, pastors and caring others dismiss various symptoms, from blurred memory to depression, as part of growing old. Meanwhile, millions of women like Mary Ann, retreat deeper into self-imposed exile. They place themselves in prisons that can become coffins when alcohol and prescription drugs are mixed.

If you, or a friend, has become preoccupied in any way with alcohol, including watching the clock for 5 pm cocktail time, the likelihood is that there is a problem that needs addressing. Do any of the following apply?

- Abrupt or significant changes in behavior
- Insomnia or restless sleep
- Deterioration in grooming and housekeeping habits
- Previously controlled conditions via medication, now out of control, i.e. diabetes, hypertension
- Bottles stashed in the home

Like Mary Ann, other women of our generation were not brought up to deal with emotional problems. We were taught to view alcoholism as a sin or embarrassing weakness.

Few of us are strong enough to take charge of this serious problem "cold turkey." Intervention of a non-judgmental, caring person, like Vivian, is most often one's best hope of recovery. Late-onset alcoholics have an excellent chance of recovery!

Reach out. Someone needs help. Is it you?

Footnote: To get help, google **Women for Sobriety**, **AARP**, or **Alcoholics Anonymous**, known for holding meetings close to where you live. You can find all three organizations on Facebook.

Footprint: Although God is everywhere, He always places a Christian care-giver close by.

Give me the courage, Lord, to accept the caring of a sister in Christ. Amen.

Star Worship

Scripture Focus
DEUTERONOMY 17:3-5
DEUTERONOMY 4:19

KATHY FINISHED CUTTING my hair and was sweeping up when we overheard the beautician in the next booth ask her client, just seated, "Trim or full cut today, Arlene?"

Startled, I peeked into the next booth and found a lady who resembled me in size and skin coloring. "Pardon me," I ventured, "Vickie called you Arlene. That's my name, too."

Before the surprised woman could reply, Vickie chirped, "She's single, just like you. My Arlene is a school teacher. Didn't you used to teach?"

"Yes," I replied, growing cautious. Still, I was compelled to inquire, "When is your birthday?"

July 1st," she returned, dismissing our brief encounter. Then to Vickie, "How about a feather cut today?"

My mouth opened, but a strange foreboding kept me from speaking. Kathy, a Bible study sister of mine, whispered, "Go ahead. This feels like one of your God things."

July 1st is my birth date, too." I announced warily. An inner nudge pushed me to add the year.

"What time of day? I must know exactly." The other Arlene suddenly sounded driven.

"About 3 pm."

"The stars foretold a dynamic event in my life this week. Gemini is ascending – for you, too!"

"I don't believe in…" I started.

"Our lives have crossed for a reason, don't you agree?"

I definitely agreed. Kathy shot me that "go on" look.

You must meet my astrologer, Madam C'leste. I seek her advice on absolutely everything, including the future. She's told me that the stars line up perfectly for remarriage next year." She smiled, adding, "That means for you, too!"

The noise of Vickie's blow dryer kept us from further conversation. It was just as well. I needed time to think and to pray. I knew Kathy would be doing the same.

A recent Gallup Poll revealed that Americans are more likely to check their horoscope in the daily paper, than read the Bible daily. It's not common knowledge, but newspapers often assign horoscope writing to the newest staff member.

A prominent psychologist checked the records of hundreds of couples who married, then divorced. Those born under "compatible" signs marry and divorce just as often as those born under "incompatible" signs.

There is no personal power in astrology. There is no secret to success, no shortcut to love, riches or happiness waiting for us in the stars.

The Bible speaks strongly against this form of idolatry. Reading your daily horoscope or wearing zodiac jewelry, gives the devil a foothold. Satan is delighted when a Christian witnesses for him!

Let's look for guidance, not among the stars, but to the One who guides the stars themselves. Isaiah 40:26 tells us:

"Lift your eyes and look to the heavens;

Who created all these?

He who brings out the starry host one by one,

And calls them each by name.

Because of His great power and mighty strength,

Not one of them is missing."

"The heavens declare the glory of God: the skies proclaim the work of His hands." (Psalm 19:1)

Arlene and I left the beauty shop at the same time. We chatted on the way to the parking lot. It was my turn to share my Advisor's Word with her. She listened.

When we reached her car, she took out a note pad and leaning on the hood of her car, copied down several Bible references I shared with her.

"I never considered astrology in conflict with God," she confessed.

The seed was planted. I will remember to pray for her, especially on our birthday!

Footnote: This is a good time to go through your jewelry, shelf of coffee mugs and old magazines. Toss out all "signs" that glorify Satan's world of astrology.

Footprint: *Praise Him, sun and moon, praise Him, all you shining stars.*" (Psalm 148:3)

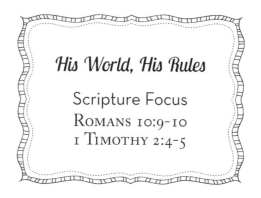

His World, His Rules

Scripture Focus
ROMANS 10:9-10
1 TIMOTHY 2:4-5

THE FRESH SCENT of dew-dipped mountain pine prompted me to open my eyes and peak out from my sleeping bag. Spiked mountain peaks jutted up from the far side of the meadow. Entwined salmon and sliver clouds stretched lazily across the morning sky.

I sat up to watch a lone fly fisherman cast his line into the glassy stillness of a reed encircled pond a couple hundred yards away. Thousands of baby grasshoppers, in search of an early breakfast, sprang up and down from the tall grass between me and the pond. Across the meadow, a fawn stood motionless at the forest's hemline, watching a bird dance teasingly above a fallen log.

I was not alone. God's creation, God's presence, was all around me.

The inhabitant wildlife of Inspiration Valley simply ignored the two dozen motor homes, vacation trailers and tents tucked around the meadow's perimeter for the weekend visit. I wondered if nature would remain as nonplussed later today, when about 400 non-campers, friends of our host, would be arriving for the private "Christmas in July," pit barbecue.

As part of this 50 year tradition, we will gather at 4 pm, to watch the roasted pig hauled from the underground bed of hot coals. The dinner bell will be rung and the guests, toting delicious side dishes, will converge at the long rows of paper-covered tables in the middle of the meadow. All, except for Ken, who died in May.

Ken was a regular attendee. He was a red-faced, foul-mouthed hard drinker, whose inflated ego and conniving schemes kept him a half-step ahead of the IRS. Six months ago, Ken became terminally ill and frightened. Remembering his Sunday school days, Ken called on the name of Jesus. God touched Ken with His grace.

The sound of a twig snapping interrupted my musing. I turned to see Jerene and her yellow lab approach my private haven. She knelt beside me and freed Brandy to chase butterflies.

I didn't see you at Ken's funeral." she started. "It was weird. Do you know what religion he got sucked into about six months ago?"

"I heard that he joined Harvest Christian."

"That was it. The service was creepy. I didn't like the narrow-minded attitude of the pastor. He didn't talk much about Ken. Instead, he raved on about faith in Jesus Christ being the only way to Heaven. Over and over! I didn't like hearing it, I guess, because I don't agree."

"With which part don't you agree?" I stretched my legs out of my cozy cocoon.

"I spend my lifetime trying to live by the Golden Rule. I should get an "A" for effort and a pass into Heaven. People like Ken, who live a despicable lifestyle most of their lives should have to answer for the misery they've caused. Agree?"

"No," I answered softly, rolling up my sleeping bag. "Look around us at our Creator's handiwork. The sun, the moon still visible up there, the changing of the seasons, the animals, grasshoppers – all created by God. All creation conforms to His rules. When God created man in His image, He gave each of us a free will. We may choose to, or choose not to, follow His rules.

"Which means…?" She treaded cautiously.

"God gave us His Word, so that we may know His Will. He tells us that *'if you confess with your mouth, Jesus is Lord,' and believe in your heart that God raised Him from the dead, you will be saved.'* "It's that simple. What you or I think should be the rule for Salvation, is of no importance."

"Well, I don't buy it!" Jerene's tone was firm. I'm still angry at the preacher for letting Ken off "scot free!"

With those final words, she got up, dusted off her pants and walked off toward the smoldering pit and its hot bed of coals. Jerene didn't take hold of the opportunity for eternal salvation this time. Hopefully, next time.

Footnote: Do not burden yourself with another's denial of Christ's gift of life. Do accept every opportunity to share the gift of enternal life. Remember, God charges each of us with planting the seed of Salvation in another's life. We may not be the one to see that planted seed grow and bloom. That gift may belong to another.

Footprint: *"He who has the Son has life; he who does not have the Son of God does not have life."* (1 John 5:12)

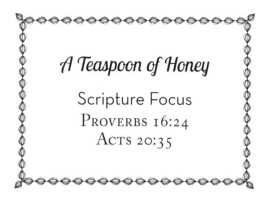

A Teaspoon of Honey

Scripture Focus
PROVERBS 16:24
ACTS 20:35

"USHERING AT A WEDDING is more than an honorary title," I smiled, making quick eye contact with each of the seven young men huddled around me in the narthex of the church. "Ushers are the first persons to greet arriving guests. You help set the festive tone for this formal event."

"How do we make that happen?" Jacob was the tallest of the groom's college friends.

Helping brides plan the perfect wedding is one of the things I enjoy most. Almost every time I coordinate a wedding, I hear that young man's question. My answer is, "Greet each guest with a smile in your eyes. Offer a genuine compliment to every lady who takes your arm to be seated. I lightly add, "Do it without gum in your mouth!"

The next question is also predictable. "What if I can't think of anything to compliment?"

"Think of her as your date. She's all dressed up and you are a handsome young man. Look at her as a precious someone you want to impress."

Later, during the reception, one of the ushers approached me. "I did as you suggested. I figured out something sincerely complimentary to say to every lady. I admit, one cranky old woman was quite a challenge. I pretended she was my grandmother. His eyes twinkled when he added, "I learned long ago how to get on Grandma's good side. All it takes is a teaspoon of honey. My dad taught me that!

"How did complimenting someone make you feel?"

He grinned. "Great! Most of the ladies smiled. One unescorted, older lady whispered, 'Thank you. How sweet of you.' She squeezed my arm. That reminded me of my grandmother."

A genuine compliment costs nothing. It takes only a moment and can be a priceless gift that lingers. I was reminded of that when an elderly lady reached for my arm as I was leaving church one Sunday.

"Thank you for sending me that pretty get-well card with sweet peas on the front. Sweet peas were a favorite flower of my childhood. I keep your hand-written note beside my bed. I reread it when my spirits need a bit of a lift."

I mailed her that card six months ago, when she had shingles. I understood her severe discomfort. I've had shingles twice, once a year after I was given the shingles vaccine!

One doesn't need to be a grandmother, or to be old, to desire to feel important, needed and appreciated by at least one person. Most of us yearn for more -- kind words from close family or special friends. Some need constant reassurance by a village! *"Pleasant words are like a honeycomb, sweet to the soul and healing to the bones,"* Solomon wrote. Women who live alone hope to hear such words for balance in their lives.

Fortunately, we don't have to wait to receive, before squelching the desire to be appreciated. There's no restriction on age to reap the rewards of being needed. We have control over how others see us!

Remember when Jesus himself said, *"It is more blessed to give than to receive?"* He was sharing with you and me, a short-cut to a richly abundant life.

For example: Last evening I stopped at the store for milk. I complimented the checker on her beautifully manicured nails. She looked pleasantly surprised. "I did them myself," she beamed.

On the way to the car, I asked the bagboy about his summer plans. He excitedly shared his hope to backpack around Europe for a month with a friend. He had a spring in his step as he pushed the empty cart back to the market.

A compliment is a taste of God's love for one another. His supply is endless. Ours can be, too.

Footnote: List six women who would appreciate a verbal hug. Call, visit or write a note. Be prepared to count your blessings ten-fold!

Footprint: *"Grant us hearts, dear Lord, to yield Thee gladly, freely, of Thine own; .... Warmed by Thee, at length believe that more happy and more blessed 'Tis to give than to receive.'"*

"Lord of Glory, Who Has Bought Us"
Elia S. Alderson, 1864

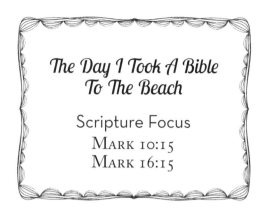

The Day I Took A Bible To The Beach

Scripture Focus
MARK 10:15
MARK 16:15

I USUALLY DON'T think of Christmas in August. However, God reminded me in a fascinating way, that Christmas is a year 'round celebration.

It began one Saturday afternoon. I pondered silently, as I folded laundry, emptied the dishwasher. I was searching for an answer to a question I had about witnessing.

Finally, I decided to set aside my household chores and drive to Moonlight Beach, praying the salt air would clear my brain. On the way through the family room, I grabbed a Bible off the bookshelf. I didn't realize until I was settled on the sand twenty miles from home, that the Bible was *Reach Out*, the children's version of *The Living New Testament*.

I began to read. Suddenly, a loud obscenity shattered my thoughts. On a blanket, a few feet away, an angry teenage girl towered over a younger, frightened boy. She snarled, "One more word and I'll slap your face!" She turned her back and returned to baby-oiling her legs.

I watched, as two other youngsters taunted the brown-eyed child, who appeared to be about eleven years-old. They mouthed four-letter words and threw sand at the scolded boy. Exasperated, the taunted boy retaliated with a handful of sand and was caught. The angry teenager lunged toward the boy with clenched fists, but stopped when she saw me rising from my blanket.

"I'm going to dig for sea shells, may I take him along? I'd like some company." I tried to hide my disgust with a small smile.

"Keep Kevin as long as you like. I hate the little brat."

We hunted shells silently for a few minutes, Kevin warily assessing me. I suspect he was mistrustful of my motive. Fair enough, I didn't know what my motive was! It all happened so fast, as if the whole cameo was not of my doing.

Gradually, with starts and stops, I learned that Kevin was in the sixth grade, got an "A" in math, but seemed proudest of his profane vocabulary, with which he salted every response.

"That kind of language won't get you anywhere," I warned.

"Wanna bet? I'm the toughest kid at Carter School."

"Yes, Kevin, I do wanna bet. What you need is love. Do you know what it means to be a Christian?"

He looked up at me with dark, empty eyes. I hurt for his loneliness. Slowly, I began to fill his thoughts with visions of God's promise woven in parables I thought most interesting for his age.

For the next hour, we strolled along the waters' edge. The roar of the ocean, the cry of the gulls, seemed to punctuate the non-stop questions that spilled from his heart -- questions like, "What are sins? Won't other kids laugh at me? How will I get friends if I don't win fights?"

We were returning to my blanket when Kevin asked, "How am I gonna know how Jesus wants me to live?"

I smiled and thought, "Jesus, now I know why You had me bring the children's version!" I handed Kevin my Billy Graham autographed copy of *Reach Out.* A moment later, he was back on his own blanket sharing the Good News.

Two days before Christmas, the phone was ringing as I unlocked the front door. My arms were loaded with holiday groceries. My breathless "hello" was not exactly filled with Christmas joy.

"Finished it!" a young voice announced excitedly.

I was silent, not connecting with the caller or the message.

"*Reach Out* – I read the whole book before Christmas. It's my present to Jesus!"

I sat down on the stairs and let the groceries bags slide to the floor. Choking back tears, I said, "Kevin, I know God is very pleased. You've given me the best Christmas present ever."

Footnote: The witnessing question that had plagued me earlier was this: Since all my friends are Christians, how does a single woman witness to strangers? I can't walk up and say, "You need to know Jesus."

Wanna bet?

Footprint: *Jesus, direct me to where, and to whom, I am to reach out to share the Good News. I am not afraid. Amen.*

And The Winner Is....

Scripture Focus
HEBREWS 15:5
MATTHEW 5:16

"LOOK AT THAT busload of blue-hairs out to gamble away their dead husband's hard-earned money!" Clarence exclaimed somewhat sarcastically, as we sat idling, waiting for the light to turn green.

I looked where he pointed, bristling at Clarence's tone and over generalization. At curbside, a tour bus was unloading older women passengers in front of one of the many Indian casinos that have recently popped up across our state.

Most of those disembarking wore white-haired poodle cuts, flowered muumuus, bead necklaces, shoulder bags and flat open-toed sandals. It's not a crime to dress for the 80s or to spend money that was legally theirs. There are no pockets in shrouds.

When the light changed, Ron turned into the casino parking lot, following the emptied bus. "Bus drivers stop for meals where the food is best. Look at that marquee – 'All you can eat-prime-rib buffet for $5.99!'"

We six, two couples and my friend Sally and I, agreed to an hour's stretch before tackling the remaining journey to our destination, a surprise birthday party. I knew how I intended to spend my free time after the buffet. Maybe Clarence didn't know everything!

While the others finished dessert, I sauntered into the casino and bought a roll of nickels. It took some searching to find the non-smoking section, a machine that accepted less than dollar bills and an empty seat at a one-arm bandit next to a poodle-cut gambler.

"You come here often?" I asked, after we'd dropped a few coins together. "Every day, 8 to 5. Free bus from town. Five years now, ever since my husband died. Lots of us here in the same boat." She glanced around the room, nodding.

"Wow," that was easily forth-coming. It sounded like what she needed most was a listening ear. "All day, every day?"

"Nothing else to do. Besides, it's hot outside. I save on my air-conditioner when I come here."

"Do you win that much?" I ventured.

"Win? Honey, you must be from out-of-town. The house always wins. How else can they afford to feed you prime rib?"

It appears Clarence might be right.

Gambling isn't nickel-and-dime entertainment. It is a major source of bankruptcy and divorce in our state. Cards, bingo, race track on/off betting, legalized riverboat gambling, fantasy football and the biggie -- state run lotteries, are all proliferating. No longer does one need to catch a bus to Las Vegas to lose a life's savings.

The gambling "take" is in the billions. Losers number in the millions. People of all ages out of control! There are no winners!

What does God say about gambling? A lot! In Exodus 20:3, He says clearly, *"You shall have no other gods before me."* Compulsion and poor use of long-saved funds makes gambling a god. The Bible tells us in 2 Thessalonians 3:12, *"to earn the bread we eat."* In Exodus 20:15, He admonishes us, *"not to steal (even from ourselves.) We are to live self-controlled, upright and godly lives,"* according to His Word in Titus 2:12.

There are no blood tests to identify a compulsive gambler. We may know women who are hiding their loneliness by catching a free bus away from reality, hoping to strike it rich in order to feel good about themselves and to be acknowledged by others.

Do you know a lonely woman, with time on her hands, who shouldn't need money for an emergency car repair bill, or needs to borrow money because her monthly check hasn't arrived? Maybe someone you've noticed with a personality change to increased nervousness or anxiety? Perhaps you know someone who displays a degeneration in work habits. The above are all red flags to a possible gambling addiction.

Take a risk. Offer a listening ear. Follow through, if needed.

Footnote: google Gam-Anon. Its website is www.gam.anon.org. The first sentence on its home page reads, "Are you alone?" The organization welcomes on-line chatting, as well as holding live weekly meetings near you. No bus needed.

"In everything you do, put God first, and He will direct you and crown your effort with success. (Proverbs 3:6)

Footprint: *Almighty and merciful God, may I cheerfully accomplish those things which you would have me do this day. Amen.*

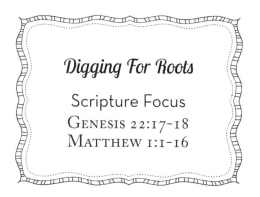

Digging For Roots

Scripture Focus
GENESIS 22:17-18
MATTHEW 1:1-16

I NEVER CARED for my middle name. I was teased by school friends who said I was named Ethel to give my father, a gasoline distributor, free advertising. My mother said I was named for her mother, about whom she knew very little.

It began when my father died and Mom was left alone. I didn't realize how unsettled Mom felt until she mentioned that the Old Testament is full of "begets" and "begots," and the New Testament begins with the genealogy of Jesus. Mom yearned for her own roots.

Orphaned as small children, Mom and her four brothers were taken in by distant relatives who had a dozen children of their own. There was no time for fireside chats about family begets and begots.

Mom loved the Lord with all her heart. She married, was fruitful and multiplied, according to His Word. What Mom didn't have was a past history. She was still an orphan. History started with her.

I have always felt connected with family. I live in the same small town where my father lived since he was two years old until his death. My children and a granddaughter were born here. My aunts, uncles and most of my seventeen first cousins live within five miles. I had no particular interest in digging deeper for my roots. That was true until my mother's seventy-fifth birthday, when I asked what she'd like as a present.

"I don't need a thing. You give me a gift and I will send five knickknacks home with you. I'm trying to downsize!"

Out of nowhere I blurted, "How about we research your family history?" I had not a clue what that meant, but Mom was pleased.

I called a friend who was deeply involved in family genealogy. I knew my grandmother's name. She was born in a town in Illinois that began with the letter "O" and had a railway station. How and where do I start? I didn't want a hobby. I just wanted to complete this one little project. I should have known by her laugh.

That was years ago. Every time I go back a generation, the number of grandparents doubles. As another wedge of US history unfolds, it opens up more personal family information. Names become real people -- pioneers of faith, hope and courage.

Mom exchanged her orphaned status for membership in the Daughters of the American Revolution (DAR). I discovered ancestor, great-grand-father Philip Hawke, German immigrant, founder of a Christian congregation in Pennsylvania, who took up arms in 1776, declaring his family's right to worship freely forever. I unearthed more great-grandfather patriots, English this time.

Finally, I became acquainted with my grand-mother, Ethel, and her mother, America Jane (who died on a 4th of July), and with the lives of ancestors marching back to the *Mayflower* itself.

When I told Mom of our membership in DAR, she blinked back tears, "Finally, I belong. I have family," she said.

Early on, I met fellow researchers with every mail query for information. Now, membership in Ancestry.com has opened a dozen other on-line genealogical opportunities, most free. Asking Google delivers up complete, well-researched family histories. Sometimes I get to tag on to a free ride, downloading information already paid for by someone else's dedicated research time. GENmatch.com has my DNA profile. This week I connected with a blood cousin living in Oregon. We have a strong chromosome tie.

God has blessed my backward glance. I have unearthed more than 300 direct-line relatives and discovered many moments of faith and courage. I've stepped into a treasure trove of history.

An unexpected gift fell my way one day, when our newly-elected County Supervisor, (his constituents number 650,000), spoke at our large Rotary Club meeting. He mentioned that his family put down roots in Connecticut in the early 1600s and have been there ever since. Only a job requirement a few years back, moved him across the country to put down stakes in my part of the world.

Just that morning, I had been reviewing a sticky situation, trying to find proof of a marriage for which no researcher has ever found. His last name, a common one, was the same as the one I was researching. Ordinarily, a long-shot. When I felt God's prodding, I knew to expect the unexpected.

After the meeting, I approached our County Supervisor and asked, "Does the name Samuel Roberts mean anything to you?"

That not-by-chance meeting brought an eighth cousin into my present begets. Several months later, we traveled together to Connecticut during the fall colors, to meet his parents, my cousins, and to visit the three towns in which our common forefathers were honored founders of Hartford, Middletown and Windsor. We headstone hunted, taking pictures of the graves of those far-distant grandfathers who fought to insure our right to religious freedom.

Hours before she touched the face of God, My mom whispered, holding my hand ever so weakly, "I can't wait to see my mommy and daddy."

I miss my mom, just like you do, or will. I find comfort in knowing that she is finally home with family, including her Heavenly Father.

Footnote: Join **Find A Grave**, online. Volunteer to help others who live far away connect with their "begets" and "begots."

Footprint: Praise God! Our lineage traces back to God's Covenant with Abraham and His promise, *"I will multiply your descendants as the stars of the heaven."* Regardless of how we are connected with past relatives, we are all part of God's family — brothers and sisters in Christ.

The Deal Of A Lifetime

Scripture Focus
Proverbs 6:1-5
Matthew 6:33-34

"May I say something, please?"

Doris directed her question to our pastor, who was standing at the podium in front of our small Bible study breakfast group. Our Bibles were opened to the book of Acts.

Pastor nodded, probably expecting a question. However, our newest widow surprised us all by walking to the front. Her cheeks were flushed. The room was unnervingly quiet.

"I have something I need to share. If I don't do it now, I'll lose my nerve." Her eyes moistened. "I love you more than my pride or I wouldn't tell you. I'm so embarrassed. I don't want it to happen to you."

Pastor reached out in his boyish manner and put a supporting arm around Katherine's shoulders. She continued, buoyed a bit by his support. "I have been flimflammed out of $20,000 by two crooks, who convinced me that I could trust them.

We sat like stone statues, mute, without expression for several seconds until we fully comprehended what she'd confessed.

How did it happen to someone we knew? Where? When? Doris didn't have $20,000 to lose.

The truth is, more money is bilked from seniors, more specifically, recently widowed or divorced women, than from any other group. Cunning con artists steal billions of cold hard cash every year from single women just like us. We don't need sizeable savings to fall into the clutches of these villains. What we women most often have in common is that we are uneducated as to how to invest lump-sum pension, IRA or life insurance benefits that become solely ours with death or divorce.

We are also vulnerable, too trusting, believing that everyone has our interests at heart. Most of us wouldn't know a boiler room operation if it was set up in our living rooms. Let's get educated! The "deal of a lifetime" is usually an old scam with a computerized new twist.

Automatic debit scam: Beware of the phone call or e-mail that states that you have won a substantial prize or cash, claimable once you've verified your social security or bank account number.

Did you get the e-mail from an African country, advising you to wire money to cover costs so that you can claim a large sum waiting for you? It's been going around for years. It would have died off by now if people didn't continually fall for it.

Have you gotten a phone call or e-mail from a family member who claims to be abroad and desperately needs you to wire money to bail him out after an accident?

The fact that scams are flooding our e-mail accounts, indicate that our e-mail addresses have been hacked by someone, sometime. Don't *ever* give or send out any personal information, especially your social security, bank account or credit card numbers to anyone you don't know*! Ever means never!*

Charitable/religious fraud: Don't feel guilty withholding a donation for from any organization that uses telephone solicitation. The organization may be upstanding, the caller may not be. Bogus charities pop up whenever there is a natural disaster – hurricane, flooding, etc. Don't be fooled by charities that want to come by and pick up your check. Real bodies don't mean real charities, no matter what the tee shirts or sides of the van read.

If you desire to have your charitable donation stretch as far as possible, check out how much money goes to administration before going to the need it advertises to serve. You will be shocked how many organizations are handsomely self-serving!

Investment Schemes: Where do you start? Should you invest in gold or silver? How about a gold mine or an oil well? Private lender trust deeds that pay high interest? Out-of-state real estate, time-shares, a friend's start up business? The stock market, mutual funds or a loan to a relative? How about a charitable trust? Should you have a trust?

All of the above may be legal. That doesn't make any of them right for you. How do you know what to do? You don't.

Trust your financial care to a professional. Word of mouth by satisfied family or friends is a good place to begin, if you don't already have an attorney, financial advisor, stock broker or banker whom you trust. Take your time. Don't let the money burn a hole in your pocket.

Footnote: Senior centers, the Better Business Bureau, reputable banks and stock brokerages, as well as adult education and community colleges offer on-going classes on seminars available to anyone interesting in becoming savvy about his/her own financial future. You may well become your own best advisor!

Footprint: *Remind me, Counselor, worry for to-morrow is not a wise investment on any day. Teach me to listen with care for Your guidance and to wait patiently on Your timing in all things. Amen.*

Join The Club

Scripture Focus
MATTHEW 25:20-21
COLOSSIANS 3:14

THOSE OF US who find ourselves alone after a long-term marriage, have more in common than an empty side of the bed. We were reared to be wives, mothers, time managers and thrifty shoppers. A greater number of us, more than in our mothers' day, stepped out of the kitchen into the workplace as co-breadwinners.

Whether our glass slippers were shattered by death or divorce, we are each suddenly faced with making big-girl decisions about a lot of things, especially about our money. Many of today's women have an acquired curiosity and ability for hands-on involvement in building their financial future.

Virginia, a legal secretary, was new to the community when she joined our church family. One Sunday morning, she asked me, "Do you know of a ladies' stock investment club I could join? I belonged to one in Seattle. It's the safest and nicest way to meet women with financial goals."

"No," I replied, perplexed. Financial goals? Aren't those for people with money? I thought about the few stocks my grandfather left me. I ignored the brokerage account, set up in my name, not knowing what else to do. "Too bad," she sighed, "it's fun to earn while you learn."

Then, almost as an afterthought, she challenged, "If I knew one other woman in town interested in her financial future, I'd start my own club."

I became "the other woman." We began our joint venture by visiting a monthly meeting of *Dollars for Dolls* in San Diego. Then we held an introductory coffee to identify ladies in our church or among our friends, who were interested in riding the ups and downs of the Dow Jones.

Surprisingly, we closed our membership with the ideal number of 15 at the first meeting. We chartered with the non-profit *National Association of Investment Corp.(NAIC),* as the *PDQs, "Pay Dividends Quick"* investment club.

Virginia and I became more popular than the local bridge marathon. Within a year, we helped organize ten clubs, 150 women, who by year's end, could scan the financial section of the newspaper as efficiently as the weekly grocery ads.

Most of the wealth of our nation is managed by women. I wonder how many of us realize it. We spent our married years mastering the art of prudent spending, with an eye on a relaxing retirement or worry-free "aloneness." That goal need not change. Accept the challenge of learning how to conserve the fruits of life's labor though wise, not risky, investing.

Each PDQer voted to "seed" our brokerage account with $200 each. Additionally, we invested $25 at each monthly meeting. Using *myICLUB* (division of NAIC) guidelines, we learned how to study, evaluate and trade quality stocks wisely. A reasonable goal was to double our investment dollars within five years.

We soon gained the education and confidence needed to take charge of our own discretionary funds. I started paying attention to Grandfather's gift. I began to treat my small brokerage account as a gifted fishing pole rather than a fish itself. The value of my account grew as I learned to invest with a new foundation of educated skills. My broader understanding of America's business world makes me feel more firmly grounded in the ability to care for myself financially. There are added dividends. Most important among them, I made several new, like-minded acquaintances, with whom I could have the most interesting conversations. Those conversations yielded compatibility on other subjects, doubling my investment in priceless companionship over the years.

Footnote: To start your own investment club, contact *Better Investing.org,* the official website for the non-profit NAIC. Invest in a year's sub-scription to *Better Investing*. Click on *myICLUB*. You'll be glad you did!

Footprint: *Lord, Giver of Life, give me the in-terest, the desire, to learn to be a wise steward of my monetary blessings, mindful always, that the invest-ment of faith in Jesus Christ as my Savior, is the rich reward of Heaven. Amen.*

Keep It Together

Scripture Focus
GENESIS 22:17
1 SAMUEL 2:30

SOMETIME AFTER Dad's "Celebration of Life," I was cleaning out his office closet when I spotted a familiar roll of frayed butcher paper standing in the back corner. For the last 40 years, Dad had spread open that roll, affectionately called the "family tree," on a picnic table at annual family reunions.

My grandparents emigrated from Germany in the early 1900s. The grand unrolling of the family record began years ago, when my dad and his siblings began to marry. In later reunions, Dad's five sisters, their husbands and most of my cousins, pushed closer to the picnic table to see their names in print along the lengthening branches. An aunt or two checked more closely, to be sure Dad had recorded all the marriages, births or deaths correctly that occurred since last we gathered.

Every entry was in Dad's handwriting – an almost unreadable scrawl in his final years. Dad considered keeping the family together his or-dained responsibility.

Carefully, I spread the ageing treasure out on the floor. Warm memories flooded over me as I traced family lines from one generation to another, recalling special childhood moments.

Aunt Bertha stopped her housework to teach the cousins finger-painting at her kitchen table. When she stirred up a batch of cookies, we were all allowed a turn to help mix the dough with our hands.

One Christmas, teenager Cousin Rebecca, "borrowed" the tractor, with razor-sharp discs attached, from her father's cow barn, while the aunts were doing dishes in the kitchen and the uncles were trading war stories in the garage.

Rebecca drove us younger, wide-eyed cousins, on a secret joy-ride through the hilly cemetery across the road from Uncle Kurt's orange grove. Cousin Rebecca discovered too late, that the tractor's brakes didn't work. We hung on to one another like fleas on a dog as we bounced over flat grave markers, careened around headstones and clipped tree branches, until we made it safely to the bottom of the hill. God gave each of us the gift of extended life that day. Our parents never knew.

I recalled with an edge of sorrow the time Cousin Billy and I hid under the stairs, greedily devouring our horde of *Archie* comic books. Who knew that one day Billy would become a rocket scientist and design the module that would put the first man on the moon? Or that he would become the hero of one of my novels? My closest cousin met God face to face last year.

I brought that precious butcher roll of memories back to my home, unrolled it next to my computer and began to computerize my family tree. Each person was assigned a number. My father's arduous handwriting was replaced with laser printing.

I entered Cousin Diana's name. Two divorces. She hadn't been to a family picnic in years. Neither had her daughters. Cousin Mary was widowed. Her son lives ten minutes from me. Our paths never seem to cross. Our children, second cousins, are strangers to one another.

Cousin Darwin. Nice guy, strange marriage. Asked to be taken off family all invitations. What's with him? What happened to in-law Tom, after Cousin Carrie was killed in a car accident? Their children are close kin.

So many questions, so few answers. I had missed the last picnic myself. Why? Did other absent cousins and I share a common denominator? Aloneness, complicated by grief or embarrassment? Worse, had we all become just a computer number to one another?

Life may no longer be the free-wheeling reunions of childhood, but we are still family. The rolled-up butcher paper began to take the shape of a baton passed to me. Someone was still needed to keep the family together. By now, my parents and all aunts and uncles had a "D" written by their names.

I picked up the phone and started dialing. I asked some cousins for the numbers of others. "We are having a special Cousins' Reunion," I began. "It's time to catch up before we are too old to remember. Please bring your memories to share."

It was a wonderful evening! We chatted until the wee hours, sharing delights and disappointments with unabashed childhood honesty. Three cousins discussed business "networking." Others talked of vacationing together.

The next family gathering was the best attended in years, the cousins stressing to their children and grandchildren the importance of keeping our six-generations of memories alive.

Reunion attendees now scan the computerized family book. New dates are entered on schedule. None of us is just a number in our family or in God's eyes.

Footnote: Do you know of a family member who is alone, outside the family circle for any reason? Reach out and draw him/her closer. Invite your kin to join in worship with the family of believers.

Footprint: "..you can have real love for everyone because your souls have been cleansed from selfishness *and hatred when you trusted Christ to save you, so see to it that you really do love each other warmly, with all your hearts.*" (1 Peter 1:22)

Bonus Time

Scripture Focus
PSALM 118:24
JOSHUA 10:12-14

I WAS AWAKE enough to hear a bell ringing and to grapple for the alarm clock. Finally, I figured out that the jingle was coming from my phone.

"God bless you! What are you going to do with the extra hour this morning?" I recognized Carol's cheery "I gotcha" tone and fell back on the pillow with a thud.

"What are you talking about? It's the middle of the night!"

"Somewhere, but not here," she giggled. "You turned your clock back an hour last night, didn't you?"

"Yes…"

"You have an extra hour this morning. Get your bones out of bed and meet me at breakfast Bible study."

"Carol, you have got to be kidding! This is the only day of the week I do not have to get up early for my Y water aerobics class."

She wasn't kidding. I got up, threw myself together and aimed my car in the direction of our church where both breakfast and Bible study were served up as one.

Somewhere along Juniper Street, my brain came out of the fog. What extra hour? 6 am is 6 am, no matter what goes on with Daylight Savings Time. I would find a way to unwind Carol's clock! More fully awake, I started playing a mind game of "what if" with extra time as I drove to church.

I still laugh at myself when I recall the entire year I thought I was thirty-two years-old. When my birthday rolled around, I realized that I was actually *going to be* thirty-two. I happily accepted the 365 days as a bonus birthday gift from God.

I can't recall, did I spend that extra time growing closer to Him? Did I spend it reveling in celebrating a year sharing His abundant joy?

Each of us has bonus time that we fritter away, not counting the 18,400 seconds handed out every four years on February 29th. I believe God gifted us the extra time the day Joshua ordered the sun to stand still.

Our former minister, insisted that sleeping more than five hours a night was wasting valuable time, time that could be better spent conversing with God, jogging or walking toward the sunrise.

I tried his suggestion a few times, though not as early in the morning. However, I was early enough to catch the glisten of dew drops, the warble of early birds and the morning splash of color above the horizon. What surprised me, was the feeling of peace I had was with Him in His garden.

I've found other ways to enrich found "bonus" moments. I carry a purse-size devotional or my read a Christian book on my Kindle during expected waits in the doctors' offices or at the car wash.

I borrow CDs from the church lending library so I can listen to Christian novels during long drives. Rather than being distracted, I'm more relaxed.

The beauty shop, traditionally a gossip factory, claims ninety minutes of my time for a permanent, thirty for a wash 'n dry. Long ago, I switched to a Christian-owned salon where uplifting conversation is always in style.

I arrived at the early morning Bible study just ahead of Carol, in time to order two eggs-over-easy before opening prayer. When Carol joined me, I whispered impishly, "Help me get used to waking up early. Join me at 6 am tomorrow morning for a jog through Kit Carson Park. We won't be the only ones on the trail! Her "thumbs up" put a smile on my resolution.

Footnote: Time is a treasure from God Himself. Keep track of your bonus minutes for one week. List how you intend to return the time to God. Peace and quiet are also gifts from God.

Footprint: *"This is the day the Lord hath made; He calls the hours His own; Let Heav'n rejoice, let earth be glad. And praise surround the throne."*

"This Is The Day The Lord Hath Made"
Isaac Watts, 1719

Join The Chorus!

Scripture Focus
I Thessalonians 5:16-18
Mark 9:23

*"Oh, what needless pain we bear,
All because we do not carry
Everything to God in prayer!"*

"What a Friend We Have in Jesus"
Joseph M. Scriven, 1856

As we sang, I raised my gaze from the hymnal to watch the returning communicants file into the pews several rows ahead. That's when I spotted Grace, a friend I hadn't seen in five years.

After the service, I found her on the patio, surrounded by a group of old friends. We reached out to one another with a warmth that spanned many years and thousands of miles to Grace's adopted home in South Africa, where she lived with her military daughter and family.

"You are still my inspiration!" I whispered in her ear, hugging her close.

"And I still praise God every morning for a case of the flu! Her face was alight with inner joy.

"Tell me one more time," I urged, leading her to a bench in the shade of a patio palm. "The details have grown fuzzy in my mind, even though I have retold your story many times. Was it eight, nine years ago?"

She laughed heartily. "Twenty-one!" she corrected, her eyes twinkling. "Rosemary, the youngest of my seven daughters, was only a year-old."

Grace started from the beginning. "I was in bed with the flu, bored silly. I decided I might as well get with the project and do a breast self-examination. I mean, what else is there to do when you're sick in bed? I found a strange lump and called the doctor. I had a mastectomy the next week."

"Remember," she continued, giggling, "we had a very young pastor at the time. I recall I was sitting on the edge of the hospital bed when he came to visit. He looked uneasy, unsure how to approach me without seeming too joyful or too maudlin.

Finally, he sputtered, "How do you feel?"

I furrowed my brow and whimpered dramatically, "Fine, except that I list a little to the left!"

When Grace laughs, the world laughs with her. When we both calmed down, I ventured quietly, "I know your husband left soon after. Did he stay home to help you through recovery?"

"Physically, not emotionally. I had been through a lot in the course of having seven babies. If I didn't know before, I found out when my plate over-flowed. I needed to lean on a higher power. No human being is capable of giving the comfort and assurance that Jesus gives."

Grace took my hand reassuringly, "The malignancy was God's way of teaching me to reach up to Him in prayer, to trust Him in everything. He knew what I didn't know. He knew that I would soon be forced to rear my girls alone. I've coped all these years because I opened my heart to God as I would to a father."

She smiled knowingly. "I've discovered the world's best kept non-secret. God gives perfect advice and free counseling, 24/7, all within a prayer's reach. With my brood, I find that I pray without ceasing!"

I hadn't thought of 24/7 in that context. I was reared, as were many of you, to pray at specific times – first thing in the morning, last thing before bed. Meal times, of course. There were extra times, especially for a sick relative, for our servicemen and for special needs, mostly my own.

The 24/7 is right on! We have the freedom to pray all day long! We can pray while walking the mall, driving, walking. I like to pray while swimming laps.

We've also been taught that prayer is a conversation with God, which means two-way communication. How many times do we pray, then go about our business without giving God time to respond? We were not trying to be rude, we didn't expect a reply. Next time, talk to God as if He is a trusted friend who listens. He will offer comfort, a solution or a sense of peace that will tell you that He will handle the situation in His way, His time.

Books have been written and Bible study outlines prepared, on the subject of "how to pray." Why? Because most of us barely scratch the surface of the power of prayer, which is so within our personal reach. As Grace experienced more than twenty years ago, all things are possible when you engage God in conversation from the heart every day of your life.

"What a privilege to carry
Everything to God in prayer!"
"What a Friend We Have in Jesus"
Joseph M. Scriven, 1855

Join the chorus today. You'll hear His voice reply.

Footnote: The next time you talk to God, ask Him for advice. Wait on Him, as the Prophet Nathan waited. God will answer. He is really beside you, guiding you with perfect direction for your life.

Footprint: *Lord, I can face the future with confidence, knowing that all the events of all my tomorrows are in Your loving hands today and always. All I need do is ask and listen for Your answer. Amen.*

"*Things Go Better With...*"

Scripture Focus
Matthew 6:32
Psalm 96:2

Remember the old slogan, "Things go better with Coke"? I recalled the catchy phrase when I found a vintage family vacation picture wedged in a dresser drawer. We were posed at a windy overlook somewhere in the Southwest. The faded picture remained proof that everyone agreed to wear our identical Coca-Cola slogan pants on the same day of our vacation. Studying that historic snapshot, I concluded Coca-Cola and my faith share a somewhat common history.

Coca-Cola began as a medicine, a cure-all for a host of ills. It was first sold as concentrated syrup, packaged in green, pint-size bottles with instructions to mix with tap water. "Coke" proved to have a "kick" that made people feel better.

One summer's day, a druggist's customer needed instant relief from a headache. He asked the soda-jerk to mix the drink for him. To save steps, the clerk substituted soda water. It tasted great! A social drink was born. The rest is history.

Today, Coca-Cola is the world's largest beverage company, producing 500 sparkling and still brands, with one billion in annual sales.

When first alone, I leaned heavily on my faith, as some leaned on Coca-Cola. It was a remedy for pain and suffering. I was a tree in winter – stripped naked, vulnerable. Praying daily gave me the "kick" I needed to feel better.

By spring, the signs of healing began to show in budding self-confidence. I began to rely on my prayer medicine less often. God's prescription for healing was filled only on an "as needed" basis.

In the sweet summertime of growing accustomed to living alone, my old personality was in full bloom most of the time. I took a vacation from daily prayer, the tonic responsible for my well-being.

It's easy for faith to become seasonal, or called upon only "as needed" for medicinal purposes. One day, I realized that it was my prayer life that had added the sparkle to my life, enrichment to my thoughts and growth to my faith. I needed a slogan for my success!

I found an index card, wrote out my slogan and taped it to my bathroom mirror. It read, "Things go better with Christ. He's the real thing!"

One day, the whole world will sing His song!

Footnote: None of us can afford a vacation from God. Place a hymn book beside your bed.

Greet each morning with a song of praise in your heart.

Footprint: *"As the morning light returns, As the sun with splendor burns,*

Teach us still to turn to Thee, Ever-blessed Trinity,

With our hands our hearts to raise, In unfailing prayer and praise."

"Every Morning Mercies New"
Greville Phillimore, 1863

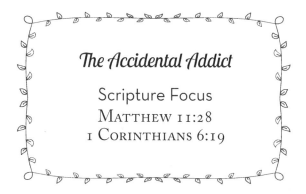

The Accidental Addict

Scripture Focus
Matthew 11:28
1 Corinthians 6:19

Like most of us in the Western culture joint pain begins too early in our adult lives. For Katherine, arthritis began making daily tasks difficult when she was barely fifty. She made the choice to sell her two-story home and move to a patio condo near the river. Members of her monthly book club volunteered to help sort and pack her belongings.

That is how, one Saturday morning, I became acquainted with the contents of Katherine's medicine cabinet, bedside drawer and the inside of several purses.

"What are you doing with all these half-filled prescription bottles?" I asked naively, as I walked into the kitchen. I held up a plastic sack of assorted bottles I had collected.

"Oh," she gulped, suddenly "busted."

Curious, I rooted around in the bag, examining the container's labels. Several medications were prescribed for a different patient, filled at different pharmacies. Most were prescribed for pain, only three had Katherine's name on the bottles, the prescribing doctor her own physician. Two prescriptions were outdated. I began to understand.

I looked up and found I was talking to myself. Katherine had bolted from the room. I found her in the bedroom, sitting on the edge of the bed, her head in her hands, crying. I sat down beside her and put my arms around her shaking body.

"It's okay, Katherine," I whispered. "The deception must be killing you inside. You can get out of this mess."

"Please don't tell anyone. They'll think I'm a junkie, incompetent to care for myself. I think people like me wind up in jail!"

Katherine continued to unloaded. "After Paul… my arthritis began to hurt more. I exercised less, ate stuff I shouldn't have. Anyway, I needed pain meds more and more often. My friend, Jessica, suggested I try her stronger pills. She also showed me how to get more pain pills without bothering my doctor."

"About a month ago, I got scared and tried cutting back to only the pills my doctor had prescribed. I got the shakes and started to sweat. Sometimes I can't sleep or keep my food down. I'm dizzy most mornings. I don't know what to do."

The answer was to "fess up" to her doctor. Katherine let me call Dr. Miller. He made time for her that afternoon. Sharing her story the second time came more easily for her. Dr. Miller explained to Katherine how she had inadvertently become addicted to drugs. She wasn't alone, he consoled.

Doctor hopping and complicated health problems compounded Katherine's fragile situation. No one was monitoring Katherine's total medical picture. Katherine had become her own worst advisor!

Dr. Miller's plan to speed Katherine back to physical, mental and emotional good health included detoxification at a gradual pace. In addition, treatment for depression was essential to prevent a relapse. He advised guidance for a lifestyle change.

"Each person is unique," Dr. Miller began. "My prescription for you is to read the Bible every day, take a water aerobics class and eat sensibly."

Then he added, "Try connecting with friends via social media or call someone who cares. Women who build healthy spiritual and social networks experience fewer diseases and live longer."

I went home and counted the pill bottles in my medicine cabinet. I found four out-of-date pain prescriptions. It is no longer safe to toss them in the trash or flush them down the toilet as they contaminate our water supply. I put them all in a bag and delivered my accumulation to our local police department for disposal.

Footnote: The assignment, should you choose to accept it, is to clean out your medicine cabinet. Make your own trip to the police or sheriff station. You'll feel better!

Footprint: *"I heard the voice of Jesus say, 'Come unto me and rest; Lay down, thou weary one, lay down Thy head upon My breast.' I came to Jesus as I was, Weary and worn and sad: I found in Him a resting place, And He has made me glad."*

"I Heard The Voice of Jesus Say"
Horatius Bonar, 1846

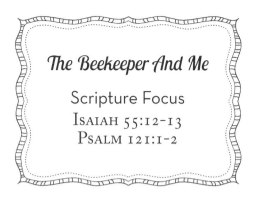

The Beekeeper And Me

Scripture Focus
ISAIAH 55:12-13
PSALM 121:1-2

GOD, THE MASTER OF SUBTLE HUMOR, is fine-tuning my attentiveness to His world around me. He communicates with me in unexpected ways. I sense it's to keep me grounded.

The latest incident began at Shelia's "Celebration of Life" service held this morning. I read the memorial folder, waiting for the service to begin. I hoped the distraction would help me forget the stack of messages collecting on my desk back at my office.

While scanning the pamphlet, I noticed Pastor had chosen Isaiah 55:12 and 13 as his text for the 90 year-old's home-going meditation. I supposed he would develop his homily around the joyful phrase, *"the mountains and the hills before you shall break forth into singing, and all the trees of the field shall clap their hands."*

Wrong. Our minister dug into tough ground, interpreting, *"Instead of a thorn shall come up with the cypress; instead of a brier shall come up with the myrtle; and it shall be to the Lord for a memorial..."*

I had known Shelia for years. She was a tireless saint. I was comforted knowing that she was free of life's stresses, released from the thorns of physical pain and the thistles of emotional battles. She was home at last, refreshed by God's everlasting peace.

After the service, I hurriedly drove back to work and to the stress headache beginning once again. As I rounded a blind curve, I braked, suddenly slowed by a stake truck ahead loaded with bee-hives. Beekeepers do not transport hives in the daytime! In that instant, came the knowledge that God had slowed me down to teach me another lesson! "Here we go again," I smiled to myself.

I hadn't seen a beehive in years, that is, until the Saturday before, when a friend invited me to ride along to the top of Mt. Palomar, about an hour north. My list of "must-dos" was already longer than my day. I couldn't go. I shouldn't go. I did go.

I assuaged my guilt by taking notes of every-thing I saw along the way up from sea level to almost the 6000 ft. level. It was an absolutely gor-geous day. I felt relaxed, rejuvenated. When I re-turned home, I tossed the journal into my purse, a little curious as to what was to become of my scribbled notes.

I was jolted back to the moment. The truck ahead stopped short. Just as suddenly, I knew

Saturday's journal notes and today's memorial text somehow belonged together – together by God's design for me!

I eased around the truck on the right and pulled into a roadside café's parking lot. I dug for my notebook to review my journal's scribbling.

As I read, I was transported back to switch backing up the narrow mountain road, passing Lizard Rocks Lane and breathing in the sweet aroma of orange blossoms drifting from local citrus groves.

I recalled vividly the field of prehistoric looking artichoke plants gone to seed and a still-life panorama of beehives stacked askew against a backdrop of rusting smudge pots.

Magenta bougainvillea splashed a welcome along the roadside at the base of the mountain. I admired the pin feathers on a red-tailed hawk lofting a dozen feet off to my right as we reached a mile above the valley floor. Together, we rose quickly through a gray, cloudy film into the summit's sunshine.

I closed the journal and listened to the words, *"the mountains and hills before you will break into singing."* God was using the verse from Shelia's service to remind me of my need to relax, draw strength and peace from His orderly creation, from the birds to the bees. God is keeper of the universe. He's my keeper, too!

Footnote: Take a break and a notebook. Seek a healing peace and perspective in God's garden. May the peace that passes all understanding be opened wide as the gates of Heaven!

Footprint: *I praise You, Creator-Comforter, for mountains that rejoice because I am not dead, but alive in You today and forever. I claim Your garden promise as my sanctuary for rest and restoration. Amen*

"Grandsmothering"

Scripture Focus
1 CORINTHIANS 12:8-10
MARK 10:13-14

ANNA B. WARNER, prolific children's hymn writer, in 1860, wrote the lyrics, *"Jesus loves me! This I know, for the Bible tells me so!"* Brings back memories of our first Sunday school experience doesn't it?

Therefore, it should come as no surprise that God would lead a little one to remind me that I am not alone and that I have a place in His family.

My oldest grandson was almost four years-old when I became single again. He lived with his parents about three hours driving time from where I lived. The distance would make it seem far enough removed from my life-changing trauma to little affect his life.

One day, my daughter and her husband took their son to the local community fair. My little grandson, Trevor, walked around the fairgrounds with three fingers on his right hand extended and his thumb and index finger tucked under. When he had trouble juggling a hotdog, my daughter asked Trevor, "What are you doing with your hand?"

His reply was matter-of-fact. "There are four people in our family. Three people in our family are at the fair. Bama is not here so her eyes are hiding."

My grandson had emotionally moved me into the circle of his immediate family. The privilege accorded me by that young tender heart is as awesome to me today as on the day I first heard the story. A grandmother alone need not be a lonely grandmother. A grandmother, though, eager to be part of a family's inner circle, would be wise to apply a balance of privilege and responsibility.

Good Table Manners for Grandmothers

Eat with your mouth closed: Do not pour out your problems on your children and grandchildren. Your family will savor your company most when your conversation is flavored with humor and good will. Also, it is easier to listen to others input when one's mouth is not in motion.

Do not stir the pot unless asked: Try to be objective, presenting multiple-choice solutions if pressed for an opinion on family matters. It is wiser to season with suggestions than to grate with insistence when in someone else's kitchen.

Accept that there is more than one way to stir the broth:
There are other rituals in the way to handle mealtimes, bath and bedtimes than when I was

rearing my family. Admittedly, other approaches could be improvements. House rules, especially those concerning the dispensing of discipline and sweets, are not to be challenged by a visiting grandmother. I am continually amazed how smoothly life goes on around me when I step aside and play mother's helper rather than mother's keeper.

Aspire to be a gourmet grandmother: Share affection liberally, equally and openly, without ties that bind. Give gifts that suit the desires and personality of the grandchild and parental approval. Costly or controversial gift ideas need to be cleared with the parents before you go shopping.

When your visit ends, walk away confidently, your heart brimming with a wellspring of kindred love. The sweet taste of success will keep you wrapped in mutual love until your next welcomed visit.

Footnote: *Grandmother's Dessert:* Offer your lap for snuggling, the cradle of your arm for comforting and your shoulder for leaning. Teach love by giving it, appreciation by showing it and the power of prayer by sharing it.

Footprint: *Lord, teach me to be a grandmother who is sensitive to my family's needs and desires. Guide me to focus on giving rather than receiving. Amen.*

Skylight To Heaven

Scripture Focus
EPHESIANS 6:2
JOHN 8:12

IT'S A GOOD THING I refilled my blood pressure medicine!" Pat exclaimed as she burst into my office. "Now we've lost the skylight!"

"The what?"

"The skylight in the church kitchen. The building committee promised our women's group a skylight if we agreed to work in a kitchen without windows. The walls are needed for cabinet space." Pat raced on. "I just came from the construction site. The heat pump for the entire complex has been installed on the roof where our skylight was to go!"

"Have you talked to the contractor or the chairman of the building committee? Certainly, they'll listen."

Pat's frustrated look was its own reply.

We both knew the conflict was not over adequate lighting in the women's work place. It was about the lingering attitude that devalued women's place in God's order. Consideration toward the fairer sex's place and projects was not a priority in what some considered "a man's world."

Learning to live on our own often finds us in a head on collision with traditionalists, who believe a woman's primary role is to be supportive and sacrificial. Most of us were reared in homes where gender equality was not considered Biblical. It was not a premise we dared question growing up.

As adult women alone, we appear to be easy prey as we nudge our way into a new era in our lives. Like it or not, we have no choice but to step up and accept an assertive role in business transactions involving us personally. The alternative could be to allow ourselves to be gouged by repairmen, salesmen and service providers. Witness the number of classic stories of women, who in this day and age, are still being taken advantage of by salesmen who exude a "trust me" demeanor.

As an aside, many of our married "sisters" suffer gender disparity as well. They could be unaware of it. Just this week I watched a television segment produced by a major network exposing an unlikely scam that has spread though the dry cleaning industry in New York City. The station sent a professionally dressed woman into several NYC dry cleaners with items to be cleaned. The station then repeated the process with a professionally dressed man with exactly the same items to be cleaned. In every case, the woman was charged from 50% to 100% more for the same service.

Those of us who are no longer under society's perceived protection of a husband are now fore-warned of gender inequities, giving us a definite edge. We are free to embrace, rather than shrink from the liberation that comes with our new role in life. We can take on every challenge with open-eyed resolution. Armed with prayer, we may seek counsel outside our home from people wise in their fields before making any major decision ob-ligating joint or family money for major purchas-es or commitments. We have the opportunity to learn as we go. What a blessing!

Those of us making our own way in the world cannot afford to be encumbered by the added yoke of past attitudes. Neither are we obliged to fall in lock-step with every feminist manifesto. Even if we consider ourselves "liberated" women, the ma-jority of us would find it equally uncomfortable marching in a feminist parade.

In the collision, where does today's woman stand in the light of Scripture? What does God expect of the liberated woman? Of me, in particular?

Jesus revered women. For example, Jesus cut through the tradition of His day when He talk-ed about spiritual matters with the woman at the well. He ignored taboos and healed the woman who had been bleeding for years. He accepted the gift of expensive perfume and tears to wash His feet, from a woman of marginal character.

Did you know Jesus accepted financial support from women who had their own money? (Luke 8:1-3) Remember the story of the widow's mite? She was Christ's example of humility and generosity.

Jesus encouraged women to set spiritual priorities above household chores. Jesus scolded Martha for being too busy in the kitchen. Her place was with Mary, at His feet, learning His direction for her life.

Women were with His entourage and among His closest followers. He often spun parables around the daily lives of women. Women wept for Him at the foot of the cross. While life drained from our Savior's body, Christ showed His honor for women when He placed His own mother in the care of His best friend. Women perfumed His body in the tomb. Then on that glorious Easter morn He revealed Himself to two women and sent them ahead to witness His resurrection to His disciples.

Christ is not only our Savior, He is our Liberator! The "Light of the World" freed us from Satan's bondage. We are free to seek our identity in Christ, the Liberator of all who seek Him first, rather than in roles designated by man. We have status, we have authority. We are free, along with the male gender, to sacrifice and to serve others.

We are free to reach through every skylight to hold fast the promise of the rewards of Heaven.

Footnote: Women living today in countries where the gospel of Jesus Christ is allowed, enjoy personal and religious freedoms denied to our gender in so many parts of the world. We are free to worship, share our faith, express and act upon our hopes and dreams. We have equal rights under the law of our land. We are richly blessed. Pray earnestly for the women of the world who have little hope of a skylight. Pray for those who must worship in secret, live in servitude.

Footprint: *Light my way, my Savior, my Liberator. Keep my sights on Heaven as I enjoy an abundant life through loving service to others. Amen.*

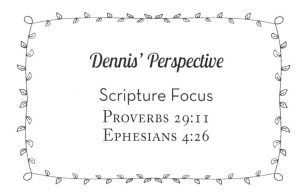

Dennis' Perspective

Scripture Focus
PROVERBS 29:11
EPHESIANS 4:26

THE EVENING PAPER was nosed into a nest of leaves near the street. I scooped it up and quickly turned to the comic section. *Dennis the Menace* has a way of placing life's dilemmas in perspective.

Tonight's slice-of-life cartoon pictured Dennis standing on the front step against a backdrop of leaves falling from a half-stripped maple. Dennis looked as if he were falling apart, too – holey jeans, bruised elbows, dirt-smudged face.

Dennis looked up at his mother. "Whew! Today wasn't what dreams are made of."

My musing was interrupted by a neighbor driving up to the curb and tapping the horn. "Hi, Jessie," I called, approaching the passenger side window. Her face was swollen and blotchy. It took me a moment to gather in the unexpected scene. "Is everything okay?"

"No!" she snapped. "I'm even too angry to wallow in my own hurt feelings!"

I opened the door, sliding in beside her. Large raindrops began to splat lazily on the windshield. "What's the matter?" I asked.

"My confirmation to serve on a community service board was blocked by a board member named Herb Knight."

"Didn't the other board members speak up for you? Who is Herb Knight? What's his problem?" I fired the questions rapidly.

Jessie's eyes flashed painfully. "I asked those same questions of my friend, Valerie, who serves on the board. It seems Mr. Knight is my ex-husband's accountant. Knight opposed my appointment because his client told him that I am a 'despicable woman.' The board, not wishing to embroil themselves in any small town pettiness, decided to take the high road and select someone else."

Angry? Jessie had every right to feel angry – toward her ex-husband, Herb Knight and toward board members who permitted the stain of false witness to influence their votes.

Anger has its place. Jesus himself became angry when he found money-changers in the temple. It is important how we handle this God-given release valve. King Solomon advised, "A fool gives full vent to his anger, but a wise man keeps himself under control."

Anger swallowed does not metabolize. Instead, it gnaws at one's good disposition. Sometimes, festering anger burrows so deeply that it causes physical or emotional illness. Negative feelings can prevent emotional healing and often hinders the expression of positive love and compassion for others and for one's self.

We cannot control the words or feelings of others, no matter how unjust they may be. God expects us only to take charge of our own feelings and words.

"What do you think I should do? You are more clear-thinking than I am at the moment," Jessie added.

I thought for a moment. "Let's regroup first. You recognize the cause and accept that you are entitled to righteous anger. That's a healthy beginning. You've shared your nightmare with someone you trust. You do not have to carry your burden alone. The next step is to do something productive with your anger."

"I can't confront anyone on the board without appearing to be what Mr. Knight believes me to be." Tears welled-up in Jessie's eyes.

I glanced down at the newspaper clutched in my fist. Dennis' perspective looked back at me. "Jessie," I began slowly, sometimes when things don't go right, justice is best served by simply releasing our anger to God's care and moving on." I showed her the cartoon.

Jessie took the paper and read the cartoon through glistening eyes. She pointed to the wet windshield. "I guess I needed a reminder that life is a little like rainbows. It takes both sunshine and rain to make them realities."

Tomorrow's clear skies will bring new expectations and a fresh perspective on life in the real world.

Footnote: Ask God to carry the burden of your anger. He's waiting.

Footprint: *Lord, make me slow to anger and rich in love. Amen."*

The Queen of
More-Than-Everything

Scripture Focus
JOHN 15:16
GALATIANS 6:9

"ONE CAN'T BELIEVE impossible things," said Alice. "I daresay you haven't had much practice," said the Queen. "When I was your age, I always did it for half an hour a day. Why, sometime I've believed as many as six impossible things before breakfast."

Alice and the Red Queen in *Through the Looking Glass* were discussing the impossible. A silly conversation on the surface, but it reminded me of women who are full-time caregivers and do impossible things twenty-four hours a day, every day.

More than 15 million Americans, mostly women, provide unpaid care to a person living with Alzheimer's disease or another dementia. Perhaps you are one of God's special angels caring for a spouse, mother or other relative. If so, most likely you have given up a career to give care.

God bless you. Only in the last few years has the general population come to realize what you cope with on a daily basis - - incontinence, agitation, memory problems, belligerency, wandering, aggression, feeding, toileting, dressing, bathing and so much more.

Alzheimer's disease is called a family disease, because the chronic stress of watching a loved one slowly decline affects everyone. Although the disease affects most people after the age of 60, it's not unusual for symptoms to appear in people in their early 30s. The younger the victim the more unlikely the person has insurance to cover institutional care.

Are you the designated caregiver in your family? If so, take stock of the people, services and information that will help you provide care. Most important, you must take care of yourself, including scheduling others to cover for you on a regular basis. President Ronald Reagan realized early on that he was entering that "long sunset at the end of life."

Care giving can last for years. Caregivers are understandably torn by the unplanned, unwanted changes in their own lives. They are courted by stress, guilt, frustration and exhaustion. Then, one day, things can begin to crack for "all the king's horses and all the king's men."

For those of us outside the looking glass, we need to do more than wring our hands in sympathy. It's not too late for us to help put things together again.

How? *"Carry each other's burdens, and in this way you will fulfill the law of Christ."* (Galatians 6:2.) We can give care to the caregiver by helping meet *her* needs – physical, personal, emotional and spiritual. For example:

Physical: Offer your hospitality in *her* home. A casserole and salad supper delivered in disposable containers would be a God-send. Check dietary requirements ahead of time. Or, invite yourself for a salad-dessert luncheon. Plan a menu that can be prepared ahead and transported easily. Tuck in a linen cloth, napkins and a rosebud from your garden. Add your company for conversation and you will be a presentation fit for the queen!

Most caregivers get short shrift on sleep. Offer to sit a few hours so that the caregiver may take a nap, take a walk or simply take a break. You can take a book if your charge is napping, too.

Personal: Many caregivers are housebound and are seldom able to arrange time for dentist, doctor and hair appointments. Make yourself available when the caregiver can get appointments. Or, you may find it mutually more comfortable if you offer to run errands to the pharmacy, cleaners or grocery.

Emotional: Keep the caregiver in the loop of life by calling or visiting with the latest news about mutual friends. Be sure she is comfortable taking time at the moment you call or arrive. She may rule the realm, but a caregiver's schedule is never her own!

Listen! Every caregiver needs someone to whom she can let off steam. Respect her trust by remaining non-judgmental and keeping all conversations confidential.

Spiritual: For caregivers, the hope of Sunday fellowship may have to await the Second Coming. Meanwhile, a caregiver's burden would be eased by one-on-one personal Bible study and tapes of Sunday services. Remember her birthday with a gift subscription to a favorite Christian women's magazine, daily devotional book or calendar.

Footnote: Feel like a queen every day. Care for a caregiver. Remember caregivers in prayer when you approach the Throne of Heaven! They are God's angels in the flesh.

Footprint: *"Let us do good to all people, especially to those who belong to the family of believers."* (Galatians 6:10)

Living, God's Will

Scripture Focus
EXODUS 20:13
1 CORINTHIANS 3:16-17

"How should we prepare for winter survival?" I asked. Most of the students stared back at me, wondering, I'm sure, where I was headed. Winter is not a survival event in the eyes of the younger generation. For them, it's snowflakes, sleds, wet socks and Christmas.

Finally - "Store acorns!" Came a shout-out. The rainy day class of characters was off and running. While one of the students transcribed practical suggestions on the chalk board, I began to seriously ponder my own question. Am I prepared for winter survival? Are you?

Looking back, I find nothing I experienced in childhood or in young adulthood that could have prepared me for survival in the winter season of life in today's world.

God's plan and mankind's selfishness are on a collision course. Women alone, especially, need to be alerted to an insidious danger snowballing through our society. Five states so far, have passed laws that allow someone to play God, assisting another person in committing suicide.

It's called *euthanasia* or *Death with Dignity.* A woman alone, without family support to see to her care or comfort, can easily fall victim to euthanasia, the synonym for mercy killing.

By legal definition, *euthanasia* means killing a human being, whether the patient is suffering from terminal disease or simply viewed as better off dead. Death may result from an action, such as giving a lethal dose of a drug, or it may come from inaction, like deliberately withholding ordinary care necessary to sustain life.

Those favoring euthanasia try to mislead, saying that God gave us free will to make our own decisions. It is only logical, that free will should extend to the decision of the value of life and death. Once a person decides he/she wants to opt out of all future pain and suffering, those who assist in the suicide are guiltless of any crime, according to zealous proponents of "death with dignity." Unfortunately, more and more states are adding some form of euthanasia to ballot propositions in up-coming elections.

Listen to these women, discussing this frightening topic over coffee. From Claire, "I don't want to be a burden to my children. When that day comes…"

Kay took her stand. "Advanced medical science has learned to save lives. The tragedy side of the mask is one of prolonged suffering for the dying. Life without quality is no life. It's my life. I will decide."

Mary Ann waited until the group was quiet. "I fear going to the hospital as I have no one to speak up for me. How dare a doctor or a committee place a price tag on my worth, my life! I panic at the possibility that God's voice will not be heeded in respect to my life."

With that said, Mary Ann pulled a printed card from her wallet. It was a quote from Jeremiah 29:11. *"For I know the plans I have for you, declares the Lord, plans to prosper you and not to harm you. Plans to give you hope and a future."*

"Only God knows when my witness here on earth is completed," Mary Ann concluded, put the card back in her wallet.

Claire spoke up. "It's the insurance companies who decide…"

Elizabeth spoke fearfully. "All my scheming daughter-in-law wants is my money. My son is vulnerable under stress. She'd convince him that I wouldn't want to live with pain."

Doctors, relatives, insurance companies, New Age cults – there's enough credit or blame to go around. It doesn't change the truth. Inducing death is contrary to God's Word and cannot be condoned or justified. Murder is murder.

We, you and I, are created in God's image. Our lives have value, regardless of what we consider as "quality."

God alone has the right to decide when life in this world should end. For us to claim the right to die on our own, or to play God with another's life is nothing less than murder! There's no mercy in Hell for those who wish to play God.

Let us return to the prospect of winter to one of glorious anticipation. Let us say with David:

> "But I trust in you, O Lord;
>
> I say, 'You are my God.' My times are
>
> In *Your* hands."
>
> (Psalm 31:14-15)

Footnote: Looking for an important ministry? Choose life! Be encouraged by the Christians who are fighting the passage of *Death with Dignity* laws in every state. Join the resistance! Enlist your Bible study group. Talk to your pastor. Take action. The life you save may be your own!

Footprint: *"Indeed the very hairs of your head are all numbered. Don't be afraid; you are worth more than many sparrows.*

> (Luke 12:17)

"The Lord gave and the Lord has taken away; may the name of the Lord be praised."

> (Job 1:21)

The Tinfoil Star

Scripture Focus
ISAIAH 9:6
MATTHEW 2:2

REMEMBER WHEN the magic of Christmas began the day *after* Thanksgiving?

That's when merchants turned downtown into a holiday wonderland. A tinfoil star shone from atop the community flagpole. Christmas carols played from hidden loudspeakers. Store windows were trimmed with evergreen garlands entwined with colored lights. Snowy cotton batting, silver sprinkles and angel hair spun an ethereal charm over window displays of crystal-faced clocks, cameras and upright vacuum cleaners.

Wide-eyed children peered through toy shop windows to watch Shirley Temple, dressed in red velvet, spin on a musical pedestal. Tinker Toys spilled out of familiar cylinders into constructed Ferris wheels. Electric trains raced through tunnels and over bridges.

Today, autumn leaves are still turning color and Halloween carnival booths are under construction at the elementary school down the block.

Nevertheless, this morning's newspaper carried pre-Christmas advertising. Cartoon videos, talking robots and electronic games have replaced dreams of dancing sugarplums.

To many of us living alone, the security of childhood sights, smells and things to-be-counted-on, belong to memories of "Christmas Past." It's easy to feel unsettled by the early advent of a season that treats tradition so blithely, until we recall the significance of the tinfoil star.

The star that shone over our hometown those winter evenings of our childhood guides us still. Its light lingers purposefully in our memories to remind us of the season's true message as foretold first in Numbers 24:17: *"A star will come out of Jacob; a scepter will rise out of Israel."*

The government, retailers and church bodies do battle in the media over the "correctness" of Happy Holidays versus Merry Christmas and the right to display the manger scene on public property. There's no doubt "Christmas Present" as we know it, is in peril. More unsettling is the thought that "Christmas Past" may never return, may never again fill young heads with Christmas carols wafting from class floats during the annual Chamber of Commerce Christmas parade.

What remains true and constant is the significance of the star that led the shepherds and Three Wise Men to the Holy manger centuries ago. God's promise of Salvation through Jesus Christ shines a brightly today as it did fifty Christmases ago.

The tinfoil star of yesteryear still lights the way, from the "First Christmas" forward to the greatest Christmas of all – the Christmas when God's magnificent gift to the world, Jesus Christ, returns to invite us home for an eternal celebration!

Footnote: Let your light shine! Dust off the boxes of "Christmas Past" decorations. Display them for friends and family. Invite the little ones to "Come unto Him" through your memories.

Footprint: *"O, star of wonder, star of night, Star with royal beauty bright, Westward leading, still proceeding, Guide us to thy perfect light!*

"We Three Kings"
John H. Hopkins, Jr.

Making Changes

Scripture Focus
ECCLESIASTES 3:1-15
JOSHUA 1:9

REMEMBER THE DAYS when a little girl's favorite companion was Raggedy Ann? Remember when a mother's significant worries were tainted canned foods and ration stamps? Remember when recovery from most illnesses was trusted to chicken soup, honey and lemon and smelly mustard plasters? In our lifetime, diet cola has replaced sarsaparilla, mutual funds have replaced the cookie jar as a savings place and inoculations have replaced the threat of most childhood diseases.

Ben Franklin reminded us more than two hundred years ago that "nothing is certain except death and taxes." Changes in life should be expected. Most changes we experience are beneficial, making daily living far more comfortable than when our parents grew up. However, the older we become, we hesitate to allow change of any kind of change into our lives. The fear of change begins to gnaw at the edge of our comfort zone.

Learning to live alone opens Pandora's Box, releasing new concerns into our sphere. Should I take in a roommate? Share my home with a companion? Should I sell and move closer to family? Should I move in with family? Can I afford to stop working? Do I need to take a job to avoid poverty? Avoid boredom?

Not all changes happen outside our personal space. All we need do is look in the mirror. Eventually, most of us see our mothers looking back at us. If only they could speak out to us, warn us of Satan's creeping assault on our aging comfort zone.

The lazy summer of our lives has barely cooled when touches of a crowning frost forewarns us of continuing changes ahead. However, the loss of a spouse, however or whenever it happens, is a sudden life-change for which no woman is fully prepared.

We begin to hunker down, to become a tad fearful, less confident of our ability to control our world as we've known it. Then, one day, total maturity sets in. We realize that we Weare not in control! We have free will, true. Free will and control are not synonymous.

This is the moment to use our free will to anchor ourselves to God's word. He spoke of change as a normal part of life. David was inspired by God to write:

"As for man, his days are as grass:

As a flower of the field, so he flourisheth.

For the wind passeth over it, and it is gone:

And the place thereof shall know it no more."

(Psalm 103:15-16)

God created the sun that nurtures life, the moon that controls tides, stars that guide men's journeys, clouds that catch shadows and fog that confuses and diffuses. God also created icy winds, heaving snow banks and raging flood waters. He prepared every creature with the ability to adapt and thrive. Then would He not, who watches over the lilies of the field, bless us with the ability to grow with change?

We fear change because we are unsure of the future that change may bring. It is easy for me to fall into Satan's snare and believe that I am in control of my daily life. That's time for a reality check. Time to reach for Proverbs 3:5-6; *"Trust in the Lord with all your heart, and lean not unto your understanding. Acknowledge Him in all your ways, and He shall direct thy paths!"*

We can trust our walk beside God because change never affects the Word of the Lord. "The grass withers, the flower fades; but the word of God will stand forever." (Isaiah 40:8) His faithfulness endures forever. Therein lies our strength.

God often uses humor to get me back on track. Remember when bumper stickers were so popular? I was on my way home from the doctor's following my annual check-up. He suggested an additional blood test. I was hardly aware of the traffic around me as I worried about the possible changes in my future. Suddenly, a driver pulled in front of me. I was forced to look at his rear bumper sticker. It read, "If God is not in charge, who fired him?"

Footnote: Name three changes you have made recently in your daily living habits. Do you count those changes as blessings? If not, do so. If so, how has your character been strengthened by each change?

Footprint: *"In Thee I place my trust, On Thee I calmly rest: I know Thee good, I know Thee just, And count Thy choice the best."*

"My Spirit on Thy Care"
Henry F. Lye, 1884

Be Gracious

Scripture Focus
PSALM 119:58
PROVERBS 22:11

I ENCOUNTERED MARK in the deli section of our local grocery store. Recently separated from Katie, Mark left on vacation and missed a family wedding. He asked about the event.

"It was a beautiful service," I replied whimsically. Katie served the cake. She looked lovely in her new dress."

"As good as anyone can look wearing a tent!"

Ouch! That hurt. And my name isn't even Katie.

Cutting an ex-spouse to ribbons is painful for everyone who hears it. It wounds the credibility of the speaker. Don't do it. *Be gracious!*

Donna, recently widowed, confided, "Howard rarely paid me a compliment or voiced approval of anything I accomplished. He constantly criticized me in front of others. Now that he is gone, I am free to be me. I don't know who "me" really is. How do I change the image Howard painted of me to others?"

Be gracious!

Years ago, a friend who hadn't seen my mother for some time exclaimed, "Why Leona, you've lost weight!"

Mom replied, "I'm trying, always trying. I doubt I'll ever be skinny again!"

My then five-year old son, Jon, put down his Match Box car, climbed onto his grandmother's lap and gave her a hug. "That's all right, Grandma. I like you puffy." That's graciousness!

Graciousness is a gift of God. Some people, like Jon, manifest it early in life and wisely cherish it. Others never get the hang of the basic concept of "do unto others…" Graciousness, like a regal bearing, is easily recognizable in those who possess it.

A gracious person is one who displays the characteristics of the Christian qualities of kindness and courtesy. Of the forty-two times "gracious" appears in the Bible, it rarely appears without the added words "and compassionate." Most everyone is lonely at one time or another. Most every person can use a bit of encouragement to add a sweet taste to the day. Perhaps, that is why graciousness is one of the most beneficial and satisfying gifts a woman alone can cultivate.

When we think first of kindness, courtesy and compassion to others, we call forth the best within ourselves and add substance to our own spirit. When we greet every sunrise with a giving heart, we are transformed. The power of graciousness becomes ours.

What a soured ex-spouse says to the world is a reflection upon his character, not on his former wife's. A woman's personality may well blossom after the loss of a spouse. How either is viewed by others will be determined by personal behavior, not by the editorial comments of anyone, living or dead.

Graciousness is more than using good manners at a Mother's Day Tea or holding one's tongue while being lambasted by a crotchety neighbor. It embraces much more.

For those of us who need a reminder course in graciousness, begin by doing something thoughtful for someone who will never discover your identity, as in paying the toll for the next person in line. It will give you the opportunity to remember how good giving anonymously makes you feel.

Stretch yourself by complimenting three people every day, beginning with the grocery store clerk, box boy or someone you see in the market. Smile.

Don't start a second table conversation when one is in progress. Let impatient drivers pull in front of you. Road rage is quite unbecoming, let alone dangerous.

Encourage hope in everyone, no matter how dire the circumstances. A soft expression, a simple touch or caring hug transfers strength to the weary in spirit. Offer to add that person to your prayer list. Be sincere or be silent. That's graciousness.

Others around you may "take the name of the Lord in vain," or dip into gutter language when telling an off-color joke. The desire to gossip is a trap of Satan to women of every language. Remember the words of King David in Proverbs 31:26, part of his description of a godly woman. *"She speaks with wisdom; and faithful instruction is on her tongue."* That's graciousness.

Footnote: Strengthen your resolve to be a gracious woman by reading Matthew 5:1-12, "The Beatitudes."

Footprint: *"The Lord make his face shine upon you and be gracious unto you; the Lord turn his face toward you and give you peace."*

(Numbers 6:25-26)

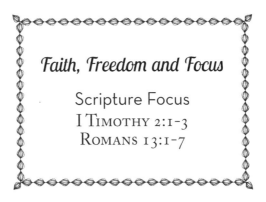

Faith, Freedom and Focus

Scripture Focus
I TIMOTHY 2:1-3
ROMANS 13:1-7

"Blessed is the nation whose God is the Lord; and the people whom he has chosen for his own inheritance." (Psalm 33:12)

WHEN I WAS a young school teacher I had no time for politics. I was preoccupied with figuring out how to stretch three pounds of hamburger until payday, how be sweet to my own children after a long day with 36 energetic 6ᵗʰ graders and how to find time to run the washer/dryer before my own bedtime. You've probably been there.

One Saturday morning, a stranger named Ruth knocked on my door with a petition for me to sign. After she explained the initiative, I told her that I did know something about the issue and was happy to add my signature.

That was the moment we became friends. Ruth, a widow within the past year and a retired teacher with a Midwestern upbringing, had reared four college-educated children. The better I got to know Ruth, the more amazed I became by her endless energy to continue to educate every acquaintance with the importance of *faith* in Jesus Christ as our eternal Savior and the blessings of *freedom* most of us take for granted. Her favorite phrase was, "Without *faith* in Christ there is no *freedom* here or in the hereafter."

Beside daily Bible study, Ruth took time to listen to several radio evangelists, write letters to her congressman and work on local election boards. She invited neighbors in for afternoon tea to celebrate our past presidents' birthdays – Washington and Lincoln.

Ruth never broke stride. At 85 plus years, with a painful gait and malformed feet, Ruth still walked her precinct, knocking on doors in a 'get out the vote' campaign, reminding neighbors of the importance of protecting the Constitution and The Bill of Rights and the *freedom* we enjoy through God's grace.

On our last day together we folded fundraiser letters at her bedside table talking politics as usual. I babbled on – about taxes going up, national morale going down, rendering unto Caesar, and the fact that there was always going to be wars and rumors of wars.

Ruth looked at me, smiling with aged eyes drained to a flat gray color. Her gnarled, arthritic fingers folding automatically and her strength weakened like her voice. Ruth whispered, "*But our citizenship is in heaven. And we eagerly await a Savior from there, the Lord Jesus Christ."* (Philippians 3:20)

I've since been able to put a name to the loving relationship Ruth and I shared for over a quarter of a century. She was my mentor. As I reflect, she has not been my *only* mentor.

June Masters Bacher was another. She was my son's 2nd grade teacher. One of her class projects was to teach her little ones how to write his/her own book. I visited her class on Parent's Day. It was then that I learned that she'd written a novel set among the fictional families of early Oregon pioneers. Believing her work not worthy of publication, she had never submitted her manuscripts to a publisher. With palatable trepidation, June handed me the typewritten original of her first effort to critique. Her characters lived lives of *faith*, exploring and living out the *freedom* found in the "new frontier,"

It took weeks for June to agree to send her first Christian romance effort to my forewarned publisher, Bob Hawkins, Sr. at Harvest House. The day June dared to "waste" postage mailing off her first novel marked the moment our friendship of mutual love and trust was forged. While millions of copies of her more than 30 books were sold over a very few years, she and I talked daily about our writing, our families.

I would drop off a manuscript in the farmer's mailbox at the bottom of their driveway. She would scan it for grammar errors then return the corrected copy to the mailbox. I would often find waiting for me in the mailbox, a list of Oregon facts to research at the library for her. Those were the days of the Selectric and before Siri. We each dedicated one of our books to the other. We mentored one another.

God's inspired Word tells us in Titus 2:3-5, that older women are expected to mentor the younger women in matters of faith and in proper daily habits. Further study finds that often younger women who are more seasoned Christians, find they have a ministry mentoring older women who are new Christians. The point is, you and I have a Christ ordained ministry among women.

Perhaps you have a younger mentor who has brought *focus* to your faith. My daughter, Alyse, has mentored me and my Bible *focus* for years. One day, circumstances brought her *faith* into the *focus* of hundreds, if not thousands of women around the globe. I am privileged to have her within arm's reach and honored to be the mother of this special woman of God.

On a Mother's Day weekend years ago, my 12 year-old soccer-playing apparently healthy grandson, Keegan, was shockingly diagnosed with Non-Hodgkin's Lymphoma, stage 4. Within three hours of his suspected diagnosis, his parents checked him into Children's Hospital in Los Angeles where he spent much of his life in and out for the next two years.

Members of our family immediately called on our combined list of prayer chains – Sisters in Service, our individual Bible study prayer chains, relatives' church prayer chains, my vast Mary Kay (a pro-active Christian company) prayer chain from customers, sister directors to national sales directors.

Six weeks later, Keegan's prognosis still in limbo, their church's pastor planned to preach on *Abiding with Him.* He told Keegan's parents that they've had many give testimonies, once healed, about the power of prayer. Would my daughter and her husband give a testimony while their son's life still hung in the balance? They spoke to a hushed crowd of hundreds. How many women do you think found a mentor by example that morning listening to their testimony of *faith* and *focus* on their Savior's promise? When questioned by Christian friends, "Why you?" Their response was "Why *not* us? We freely accept all of God's good blessings. How could we not accept the "not so good" that He has allowed." Alyse especially, found strength in Psalm 61:1-2…"*Lead me to the rock that is higher than I… "* Keegan was declared cancer-free ten years ago and recently was officially released to the care of his primary physician. Praise God!

Footnote: Ladies, no matter what our age, spiritual or chronological, we have been called by Christ to mentor other women—we live by *faith, freedom and focus.* We are all able to mentor by example. You and I have so much to offer in experience and endurance. We've trudged through dark valleys and climbed to spectacular mountain tops during our lives. It's time to reach out in joy and commitment to mentor someone waiting for you!

Footprint: *"Heavenly Father, I praise Your name, thankful for the range of experiences you have blessed me with during my lifetime. I see them now as a foundation that I may build on to mentor other women as you direct my faith, freedom and focus. Amen.*

Living Alone
Choices For Women Who Are Single Again
Notes

Single Steps Beside God

Charles Dickens, *Nicholas Nickleby*, Dodd mead, 1949, page 698.

"The Right Chemistry," *Time,* February 15, 1993, Page 49-51

The Hour In The Garden

William Wordsworth, "A Poet – He Hath Put His Heart To School," 1842

William Wordsworth, "Lines Composed a Few Miles Above Tintern Abbey, 1798

Quote used by permission of June Masters Bacher

Join The Chorus

Paul Rader, "Only Believe!" The Rodeheaver Co. 1949.

Singspiration, Zondervan, 1977. Page 425, one line.

About the author:

ARLENE COOK SHUSTER was single again for twenty years. She is an award-winning writer (1982 Writer's Digest National Grand Prize and San Diego County Christian Writers Guild 1994 Grand Prize for *Living Alone – Devotions for Women Who are Single Again*.) She has also authored several novels: *From the Ashes of Hell* (Creation House Publishers), *Forever Yours, One True Love, and Love's Destiny* (Harvest House Publishers) and hundreds of magazine articles.

Arlene Cook Shuster is a lifelong resident of Escondido, CA. She graduated from San Diego State University with a degree in Elementary Education. During her twenty 'single again' years Arlene Cook Shuster joined Mary Kay Cosmetics, one of the nation's most successful Christian companies. She travelled extensively with Mary Kay, forming lifelong bonds with many sister directors and retired as a Senior Sales Director following her remarriage.

The author has three adult children Alan, Alyse and Jon. Together with her husband Bob Shuster, they have six children, twelve grandchildren and three great-grandchildren. She and her husband are active in local politics, in the Escondido Rotary Club, as well as Grace Lutheran Church, which was founded by her grandparents in the 1920s.

Made in the USA
San Bernardino, CA
05 June 2016